JUNIOR
AND
OTHER LOSERS

JUNIOR
AND
OTHER LOSERS

PETER BAGGE

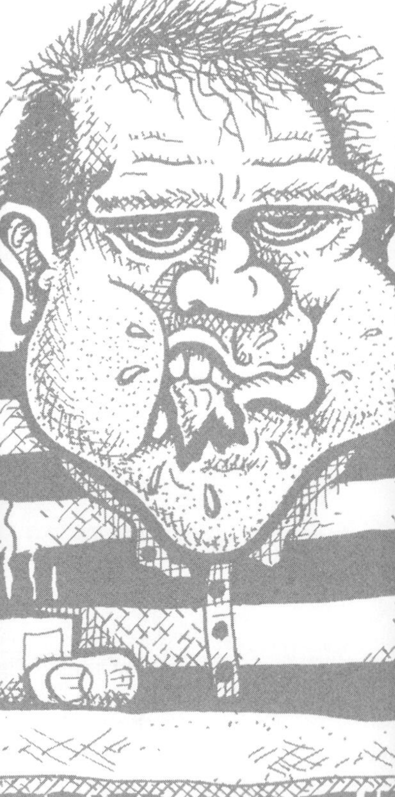

FANTAGRAPHICS BOOKS
7563 Lake City Way NE
Seattle, WA 98115

Editor: Kim Thompson
Design and art direction by Roberta Gregory and Gil Jordan
Covers colored by Monster X
Color separations by Rayson Films

First Fantagraphics Books edition: November, 1990.
1 3 5 7 9 8 6 4 2

ISBN: 1-56097-048-0

Printed in the U.S.A.

CONTENTS

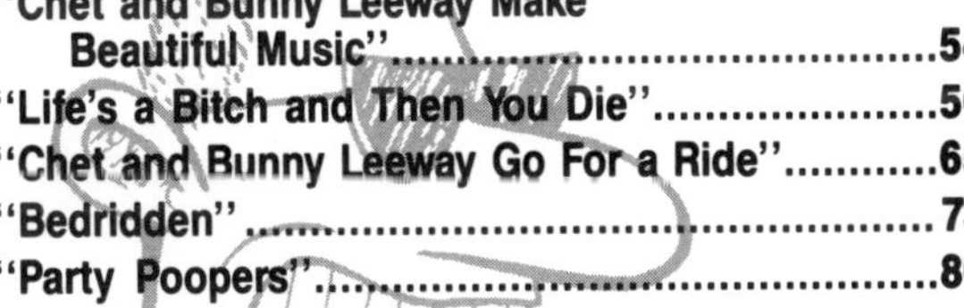

PART I

THE STORY OF JUNIOR

"IT'S A DANGEROUS WORLD OUT THERE!"

LOOK AT THE WAY THIS GUY WALKS! AND THE **CLOTHES** HE WEARS! IS HE FOR REAL?!?

LOOK AT THAT **MUG**! AND WHAT KIND OF HAIR-CUT IS THAT!? IF I WAS THAT GUY I'D **KILL MYSELF!**

JUNIOR?!? THE GUY'S NAME IS JUNIOR! MAN OH MAN, WHAT COULD BE MORE **APPROPRIATE!**

LOOK AT HIM CHECKING OUT THE LOCAL "TALENT! I'M SURE HE'S TOO **TERRIFIED** TO SAY ANYTHING TO THEM...

THOSE GIRLS ARE **LAUGHING!** COULD IT BE THEY WERE LAUGHING AT HIM?

OF COURSE THEY WERE! JUNIOR WAS "LOSING ALTITUDE"!

HE'S GOING INTO THAT DEPARTMENT STORE. LET'S FOLLOW HIM IN...
CALDOR

LOOK, HE'S BUYING THE NEW BARRY MANILOW RECORD! AND HE'S HAVING IT GIFTWRAPPED IN "GARFIELD" WRAPPING PAPER! OBVIOUSLY A MAN OF TASTE!
BAR
SING

HEY, SMART LOOKING SHORTS! THEY'LL BE PERFECT FOR YOUR NEXT VACATION IN BAYONNE!
BARGAIN BIN
½-OFF ON ALL ITEMS

NOW I GUESS HE'S HEADING FOR HOME AND... WHAT'S THIS? HE'S PICKING SOMETHING UP...

EWWW!! IT'S A DIRTY OLD M+M!! AND HE'S EATING IT TOO! YECCH! HOW DISGUSTING!!!

OH, AND OF COURSE HE'S GOTTA PICK HIS NOSE! DON'T WORRY JUNIOR, NOBODY'S WATCHING! HEH-HEH!
...DIG DIG DIG...

SO HERE'S WHERE HE LIVES - I SHOULDA KNOWN IT'D BE PINK!... WELP, I GUESS THAT'LL BE THE LAST WE'LL BE SEEING OF HIM...

NO, WAIT! HE'S COMING BACK OUT! AND HE'S HOLDING SOMETHING... A ROTTEN EGG!?! WHAT'S HE GOING TO DO WITH THAT... HEY!!!!!

SHEESH! WHAT A GROUCH!
SPLAT!
© 1984 by P. BAGGE

JUNIOR

SIGH!
HA-HA!
...WHY I OUGHTA...

JUNIOR! ARE YOU GOING TO WASTE ANOTHER WHOLE DAY JUST WATCHING T.V AGAIN?
UH-OH...

DO YOU REALIZE YOU'VE BEEN OUT OF SCHOOL NOW FOR THREE MONTHS? COULDN'T YOU AT LEAST BE OUT LOOKING FOR A JOB?!
I HAVE LOOKED!

HA! ALL YOU DID WAS ASK UNCLE SID TO HIRE YOU AS HIS ASSISTANT, BUT HE'S A BIO-CHEMIST!
HIS LABORATORY SEEMED LIKE A NICE PLACE TO WORK.

LISTEN JUNIOR, IF YOU CAN'T WORK UP THE NERVE TO LOOK FOR A JOB, WHY DON'T YOU MAKE YOURSELF USEFUL AROUND HERE! DO SOMETHING CONSTRUCTIVE!
...I SIMPLY CAN NOT STAND SEEING YOU JUST SIT HERE DOING NOTHING!...
..OKAY OKAY OKAY...

NEXT DAY...
JUNIOR! DON'T TELL ME YOU SPENT THE WHOLE DAY IN FRONT OF THE T.V. AGAIN!
NOPE!

LOOK! I DID A CROSS-WORD PUZZLE!

...AND DON'T COME BACK!
BONK!
GEE WHIZ! I THOUGHT THAT WAS PRETTY CONSTRUCTIVE!
END!
©1985 BY P. BAGGE

Junior in "the CABBAGE"

4

LATER...
...HMMMMM... PRETTY RUN-DOWN LOOKING, BUT BEGGARS CAN'T BE CHOOSERS!
ROOMS FOR RENT CHEAP!

...WELP, HERE GOES...

KNOCK! KNOCK!

YEAH?
I... UH... I... UH...
YOU WANT A ROOM? C'MON IN.

WHAT'S YOUR NAME, KID?
...JUNIOR...
WHERE Y'FROM, JUNIOR?

FROM THE OTHER SIDE OF TOWN. I JUST MOVED OUT ON MY OWN.
MOM
THE LITTLE BIRDY LEAVING THE NEST, HUH? HOW DARLING. UH... YA GOT ANY MONEY ON YOU RIGHT NOW, JUNIOR?

...W-WHY YES, OF COURSE!...
GOOD. YOU'LL BE PAYING BY THE WEEK. IN ADVANCE.

HERE YOU ARE...
THANKS! YOUR ROOM IS THE LAST ONE ON THE RIGHT, DOWN THIS HALL BUT IF THE ROCK + ROLL BAND BOTHER'S YOU, I COULD ARRANGE TO HAVE YOU MOVED TO THE SECOND FLOOR...
CLUTCH!

A ROCK 'N' ROLL BAND?!
YEAH. THERE'S THIS LITTLE ROCK COMBO THAT PRACTICES TWICE A WEEK IN THE BASEMENT. MAKES AN AWFUL RACKET, BUT HECK, THEY'RE PAYING RENT FOR IT, AND THEY'RE A PRETTY NICE BUNCH OF KIDS, BESIDES.

ANYHOW, YOU'RE A YOUNG FELLAH. I SUPPOSE YOU ENJOY THAT "PUNK" MUSIC OR "DISCO" OR WHATEVER THE HELL THEY'RE CALLING IT THESE DAYS...
NO! MY MOTHER SAYS IT'S THE DEVIL'S MUSIC!

OH YEAH? WELL YOUR MOTHER SOUNDS LIKE A SMART LADY!—HERE, HAVE A SEAT— I NEVER CARED FOR THAT HORSESHIT MUSIC MYSELF, AND MR. PEEPERS, HE HATES IT!
"MR. PEEPERS"?

YEAH! SAY HI TO MR. PEEPERS!
OH, UH... HI!
MRRRROW!

MR. PEEPERS HATES THAT HORSESHIT MUSIC! WHEN MR. PEEPERS HEARS SOMETHING THAT HE DON'T LIKE, HE LETS YOU KNOW IT! HE'LL RAISE HIS FRONT CLAWS, AND HE'LL START TO HISS AND SCOWL AT YA. RIGHT, MR. PEEPERS?
HISSSZZZ
SCOWL

I FEEL KINDA SORRY FOR THEM, THOUGH. THE POOR KIDS TAKE THEMSELVES SO SERIOUSLY, KNOCKIN' THEMSELVES OUT WEEK AFTER WEEK, BUT THEY AIN'T GOIN' NOWHERE! AND HERE I AM TAKING THEIR MONEY. OH WELL, ANYTHING FOR A LITTLE EXTRA CABBAGE!
TWANG! TWANG!
GRANNY'S PAD!
UGH!
PLINK!
BONK! BONK!
BASH!
BOOM!
YOW!
BANG!
HOWL!
BELCH!
QUACK!
THUNK-A-THANG!
UMPH!
TWITCH! TWITCH!
SQUAWK! SQUEAL!
SWEAT!

"CABBAGE"?
YEAH, YOU KNOW! LOOT! DOUGH! THE FILTHY GREEN STUFF! MONEY, YOU TWIT!
SHUFFLE! SHUFFLE!
OH.

LISTEN, YOU AIN'T ONE OF THEM LITTLE WISE-ASS SOCIALISTS THAT GO AROUND PREACHING THE "EVILS" OF CAPITALISM, NOW ARE YOU?!?
WHY NO! I... UH...

AAAHH.... I WAS PRETTY MUCH A NAÏVE JERK MYSELF WHEN I WAS YOUR AGE... I DIDN'T APPRECIATE THE VALUE OF MONEY...
... I WORKED MY BUTT OFF FOR THIRTY YEARS AT THE SAME FACTORY—THE "CHICKLETS" FACTORY IN QUEENS... I WAS IN THE UNION, HAD ALL THE BENEFITS... I THOUGHT I WAS SET FOR LIFE!...
... THEN ONE DAY SOME DANGED FOOL LIT A CIGAR — ALL THAT POWDERED SUGAR IN THE AIR WAS COMBUST!BLE, Y'KNOW — AND THE WHOLE PLACE WENT KA-BLOOEY! A COUPLE OF GUYS GOT KILLED... ANYHOW, THEY NEVER BOTHERED TO REOPEN THAT FACTORY SO I WAS OUT OF A JOB.
BEACHUM GUM
CHICKLETS
KA-BLOOEY!

...A SHORT WHILE AFTER THAT MY WIFE PASSED AWAY. SO THERE I WAS, ALL ALONE, WITH NO PENSION, BUT TOO OLD TO FIND ANOTHER JOB. I DIDN'T KNOW WHAT TO DO WITH MYSELF, HOW I WOULD BE ABLE TO SUPPORT MYSELF AND KEEP UP THIS BIG OLD HOUSE...

...THAT'S WHEN IT DAWNED ON ME....
THE HOUSE!
HUH?
?

I SUDDENLY REALIZED HOW MUCH MONEY I COULD BE MAKING OFF OF THIS OL' HOUSE! I WAS SITTING ON TOP OF A GOLD MINE AND I DIDN'T EVEN KNOW IT!
$

THE FIRST THING I DID WAS I RENTED OUT THE FOUR UPSTAIRS BEDROOMS. THEN AFTER AWHILE I REALIZED THAT I DIDN'T NEED ALL OF THE DOWNSTAIRS TO MYSELF, SO I CONVERTED THE LIVING AND DINING ROOMS INTO BEDROOMS AND I MOVED MYSELF INTO THE KITCHEN...
YOU SLEEP IN THE KITCHEN?!
MRRROW...

YEAH. HEY, IT'S FINE! IT'S A BIG KITCHEN — I JUST MADE SORT OF A "PARTITION" SO'S I DON'T GET IN ANYBODY'S WAY...
...NOW LET'S SEE, WHERE WAS I... OH YEAH! I RENTED OUT THE BASEMENT TO THOSE FUTURE SUPER STARS! (HEH-HEH). I RENT OUT THE GARAGE...

DON'T TELL ME SOMEONE SLEEPS IN THE GARAGE!
WHAT? OH NO, NO ONE LIVES OUT THERE! AN ARTIST RENTS IT OUT AND USES IT AS A STUDIO!
OH.

...YEAH...A DAMNED LOUSY ARTIST, TOO! I SWEAR THAT GAL MUST BE COLOR-BLIND! BUT SHE KEEPS AT IT, CHURNING OUT ONE UGLY PAINTING AFTER ANOTHER LIKE HER ASS WAS ON FIRE!
ART'S

SHE ONCE WAS A BOARDER HERE, WHILE SHE WAS IN ART SCHOOL. SHE USED TO MODEL FOR OTHER ARTISTS SO'S SHE COULD PAY HER RENT...
SHE USED TO POSE FOR SOME PHOTOS FOR ANOTHER BOARDER, THIS GUY NAMED LARRY SILVERMAN, WHO STILL STAYS HERE OFF AND ON. HE'S A REAL SLIME-BUCKET, THOUGH I KINDA LIKE THE GUY...
HE TOLD ME THE PHOTOS HE TOOK OF HER WERE FOR A MAGAZINE. HE WOULDN'T SAY WHICH MAGAZINE, BUT YOU COULD BET IT WASN'T FOR FAMILY CIRCLE! I JUST PLAYED DUMB TO THE WHOLE THING...
BLUSH!

LARRY SILVERMAN, WHAT A CHARACTER! HE'S ALWAYS INVOLVED IN SOME KIND OF SCAM OR SHADY RACKET. SOMETIMES IT'S GAMBLING, OTHER TIMES HE'S IN "REAL ESTATE", WHICH MEANS HE'S ACTING AS A MIDDLE-MAN FOR THE "MOB", HIRING ARSONISTS. AFTER AWHILE HE ALWAYS THINKS HE CAN OUT-SMART THE MOB, AND TRIES TO SHORT-CHANGE THEM. BUT THEY ALWAYS FIND OUT ABOUT IT, AND HE ALWAYS WINDS UP HERE, BEGGING ME TO HIDE HIM. ONCE I HAD TO CONVINCE THESE MEAN-LOOKING HOMBRES THAT HE WASN'T HERE. LUCKY FOR HIM I'M A GOOD LIAR! BUT THAT GUY NEVER LEARNS...

GOSH! HOW CAN SOMEONE LIVE LIKE THAT?
PEOPLE WILL DO SOME STRANGE THINGS FOR MONEY... OF COURSE, FOR ALL I KNOW HE MAY BE DEAD BY NOW, BUT THEN AGAIN, HE COULD COME BUSTING THROUGH THAT FRONT DOOR AT ANY SECOND...

BAM!

HIC!
IS THAT HIM?!
NAH. THAT'S JUST GEORGE. HE'S ANOTHER BOARDER.

HEY GEORGE! HOW'S YOUR LOVE LIFE?! HA HA HA HAHA!...
FUCK YOU OLD MAN!

IS HE A SLIME-BUCKET TOO?
WHO, GEORGE? AAAH, HE'S JUST A PATHETIC JERK!

HE WORKS DOWN AT THAT NUCLEAR POWER PLANT. ONLY A MORON WOULD WORK AT THAT PLACE, BUT I HEAR THEY PAY WELL, SO I GUESS IT'S THE BEST JOB YOU COULD EVER HOPE TO HAVE, IF YOU HAPPEN TO BE A MORON LIKE GEORGE.

"ONCE IT WAS **GEORGE HIMSELF** THAT CAUSED THAT PLANT TO SHUT DOWN! WHAT HAPPENED WAS HE HAD ONE OF THEM "**BONG**" THINGS—YOU KNOW, TO **SMOKE DOPE WITH?**—ANYHOW HE WANTED TO FILL IT WITH WATER, SO HE TURNED ON THIS HOSE THAT TURNED OUT TO BE SOME SORT OF **EMERGENCY VALVE** FOR THE WATER THAT COOLS THE REACTORS, OR SOMETHING.

"NEXT THING YOU KNOW, ALL THESE **ALARMS** ARE GOING OFF, AND GEORGE RUNS AWAY **LEAVING THE HOSE ON!**"

"...THEY HAD TO SHUT DOWN THE **WHOLE PLANT** FOR A COUPLE OF DAYS AFTER THAT, AND EVERYONE WAS IN A **PANIC!**

"SO DON'T THAT BEAT ALL? THE GUY RISKS **BLOWING UP HALF THE STATE** JUST SO HE CAN GET **STONED!** AND GEORGE TOLD ME THAT STORY HIMSELF — HE THINKS IT'S A **BIG LAUGH** THAT HE **NEVER GOT CAUGHT!**"

"HE'S GOT THIS FRIEND WHOSE NAME I DON'T KNOW, BUT EVERYONE CALLS HIM "**THE LEGEND**", I GUESS BECAUSE HIS **STUPIDITY IS LEGENDARY**. THIS GUY COMES OVER JUST ABOUT EVERY OTHER DAY, AND THE TWO OF THEM JUST SIT IN HIS ROOM, SMOKE DOPE AND LIE ABOUT THEIR SEXUAL EXPLOITS. THEY'VE GOT THE **FILTHIEST MOUTHS** I'VE EVER HEARD, TOO! IF MY **WIFE** WAS STILL ALIVE AND HEARD THEM TALKING SHE'D **BOX 'EM BOTH RIGHT IN THE EARS!**"

YOU SOUND LIKE YOU HATE THE GUY!
EH. I COULDN'T CARE LESS ABOUT HIM. HE HATES ME, THOUGH, BECAUSE I SORTA STOLE HIS ONE AND ONLY GIRLFRIEND AWAY FROM HIM.

YOU WHAT?!
HEH-HEH! WELL, IT WASN'T LIKE SHE BECAME MY GIRLFRIEND. ALL I DID WAS MAKE HER REALIZE WHAT A JERK THE GUY IS!

"WHENEVER SHE'D COME OVER TO VISIT HIM THEY ALWAYS WOUND UP HAVING THESE TERRIBLE FIGHTS, AND SHE WOULD COME RUNNING DOWNSTAIRS CRYING. THIS I HATED TO SEE, BECAUSE SHE WAS A GOOD KID...

..."SO WHAT I USED TO DO IS HAVE HER SIT DOWN IN THE KITCHEN, GIVE HER A GLASS OF ORANGE JUICE, TELL HER A FEW JOKES, ANYTHING TO CHEER HER UP. WE GOT ALONG WELL AND WOUND UP BECOMING GOOD FRIENDS...
TROPICANA

..."AFTER A WHILE SHE SAW LESS AND LESS OF GEORGE, AND SOON ENOUGH THEY BROKE UP FOR GOOD. THE THING IS SHE STILL COMES OVER ABOUT ONCE A WEEK TO VISIT WITH ME!"
ORANGE JUICE

WHAT DOES GEORGE DO WHEN SHE COMES OVER?
HE SITS IN HIS ROOM AND SULKS. WE CRACK JOKES ABOUT HIM AND LAUGH EXTRA LOUD JUST TO GET HIS GOAT. IF HE HAD ANY PRIDE HE'D MOVE OUT. TOO LAZY, I GUESS.

WHY DON'T YOU KICK HIM OUT?
WHY SHOULD I? HE PAYS HIS RENT. BESIDES, I'D NEVER KICK SOMEONE OUT...
NO, WAIT! I DID KICK OUT A WHOLE FAMILY ONCE!

"THAT WOMAN REFUSED TO LEAVE THE HOUSE! SHE WOULD JUST SIT IN HER ROOM ALL DAY WITH THE KID, AND CALL UP TO WHINE TO HER HUSBAND AT WORK ABOUT TWENTY TIMES A DAY...

..."THIS WOULD DRIVE THE HUSBAND NUTS! HE ALMOST GOT FIRED BECAUSE OF HER! AND AT THE SAME TIME HE HAD TO DO ALL THE SHOPPING FOR THE FAMILY BECAUSE SHE WAS TOO PARANOID TO DO ANYTHING...

..."SHE WOULDN'T EVEN GO OUT TO TAKE THE KID FOR A WALK, OR LET THE KID OUT BY HIMSELF, SO WE HAD THIS COOPED-UP, WIRED-OUT KID STOMPING UP AND DOWN ON THE FLOOR ALL NIGHT!

"THE ONLY THING THAT KEPT ME FROM EVICTING THEM WAS THAT I FELT SORRY FOR THE HUSBAND. BUT LATER I FOUND OUT THAT THE ONLY REASON HE MARRIED HER WAS SO HE COULD GET HIS GREEN CARD, 'CUZ SHE'S A U.S. CITIZEN AND HE WASN'T. SO, FIGURING THE GUY KNEW WHAT HE WAS GETTING INTO RIGHT FROM THE START, MY PITY VANISHED. OUT THEY WENT. GLAD TO BE RID OF THAT KID!

"...HIS FOLKS WERE DIVORCED, SO HE LIVED HERE WITH HIS MOTHER. HIS MOTHER WORKED LATE, WHICH MEANT HE WAS ON HIS OWN MOST OF THE TIME, SO HE PRETTY MUCH KNEW HOW TO TAKE CARE OF HIMSELF.

"...BESIDES BEING A GREAT PRACTICAL JOKER, THIS KID WAS ONE SMOOTH OPERATOR. HE WAS ALWAYS RUNNING THESE LITTLE PROFIT MAKING SCHEMES, AND HE WAS REAL SUCCESFUL AT IT. MY FAVORITE ONE WAS WHERE HE'D OFFER LITTLE KIDS TWENTY-FIVE CENTS FOR EACH COPY OF PLAYBOY THEY COULD SWIPE FROM THEIR FATHERS' STASH. THEN HE'D TURN AROUND AND SELL THE SAME MAGAZINES TO OLDER KIDS FOR A BUCK, SO I GUESS YOU COULD SAY HE UNDERSTOOD THE LAW OF SUPPLY AND DEMAND AT A VERY EARLY AGE!"
HERE YA GO, KID.
WHAT A DEAL!

HERE YA GO, MAN.
WHAT A DEAL!

AND YOU LIKED THIS KID?
IT'S NOT SO MUCH THAT I LIKED HIM AS I ADMIRED HIM! FOR ALL THE PRANKS AND SWINDLES HE PULLED HE NEVER GOT CAUGHT ONCE!

SO WHERE IS HE NOW, JAIL?
AU CONTRAIRE, SONNY JIM: HE'S IN LAW SCHOOL, WHERE HE'S NO DOUBT LEARNING HOW TO GET AWAY WITH EVEN MORE STUFF!
HEY, DON'T YOU START GIVIN' ME NONE OF THIS "HOLIER THAN THOU" HORSESHIT! THAT KID'S JUST PLAYIN' IT SMART! HE DIDN'T MAKE-UP THE RULES OF THIS WORLD, BUT HE'S WILLING TO PLAY BY THEM!
THAT KID'S GONNA GO FAR BECAUSE HE DOESN'T WASTE TIME WISHING AND PRETENDING THAT THINGS WERE DIFFERENT HE SEES THINGS AS THEY ARE AND TRIES TO MAKE THE MOST OF IT!
WHILE TWERPS LIKE YOU SIT AROUND WORRYING AND FEELING SORRY FOR YOURSELVES HE'S OUT THERE PICKIN' CABBAGE!
YOW! NOT AGAIN!

DING! DONG!
DATES?
...OOPS! MY DATES ARE HERE!
?

HOW DO I LOOK, KIDDO?
WHA?!? OH, FINE, BUT...
! ?
GOOD! YA GOTTA LOOK NICE FOR THE LADIES, YA KNOW!

I'M ALL SET GIRLS!
OOOH, FRANK, YOU LOOK SO NICE!
HIYA FRANKIE-WANKIE! *GIGGLE*

H-H-H-HOW...
ALL IT TAKES IS A LITTLE "CABBAGE", KIDDO!
DON'T WAIT UP! HEH-HEH!
WHERE TO TONIGHT: CLAM BROTH HOUSE OR CASSELA'S?
WE'LL LET FRANK DECIDE!

HUH! WHADAYA KNOW ABOUT THAT! BUT STILL, I WONDER IF HE MADE UP MOST OF THOSE STORIES,..
SLAM!

...AFTER ALL, HE DID SAY HE WAS A GOOD LIAR...

RRROW!
LEAP!
YIKES! OKAY! I TAKE IT BACK!
THE END

JUNIOR

I GUESS TODAY'S THE DAY FOR ME TO GO OUT AND LOOK FOR A JOB!

YAWN.

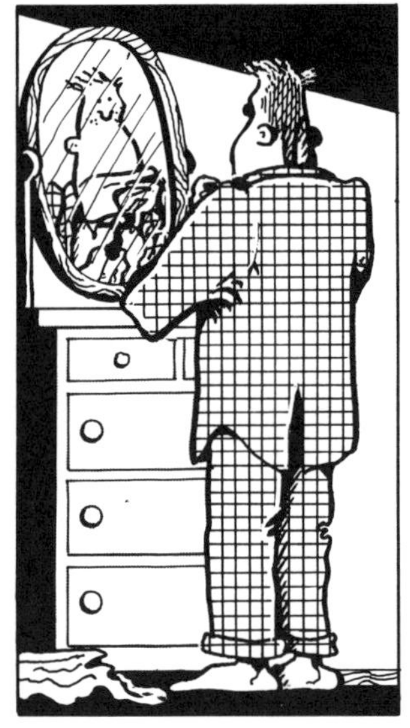

HELP WANTED

CROSSWORD PUZZLE
ACROSS
DOWN

FASCINATING MELODY...

I GUESS TOMORROW'S THE DAY I GO OUT AND LOOK FOR A JOB.

JUNIOR
RASKIN-BOBBINS
FIVE·ZILLION·TRILLION DIFFERENT GODDAMN FLAVORS!
NEW! PINAPPLE PIZZA FLAVORED ICE CREAM
5 ZILLION FLAVORS!
OPEN
NEW! SPINICH CANALOPE FLAVORED ICE CREAM
HELP-WANTED MUST BE DESPERATE
HMMM... MAYBE I'LL APPLY IN HERE...
'S MEATS
MOE'S MEATS EST. 1985
YES! WE HAVE PICKLED PIG'S FEET $6.95 lb
MOE'S MEATS
YES! WE HAVE PRESSED TURKEY LOAF – $3.95 lb
1986 P. BAGGE

ER, EXCUSE ME SIR, BUT... I... UH... I...
ARE YOU APPLYING FOR THE JOB?

YES. WELL, THAT IS, I SAW YOUR SIGN IN THE WINDOW, AND...
DO YOU ENJOY WORKING WITH PEOPLE?

PEOPLE?! WHY, YES! I... UH... GUESS .. I... UH...
WOULD YOU BE ABLE TO START RIGHT AWAY?

WHY... YES!
HAVE YOU EVER WORKED FOR RASKIN-BOBBINS BEFORE?

UH... NO.
GOOD. YOU'RE HIRED. BE HERE TOMORROW AT 11:00. SHARP.

HUH? OH! UH, YES SIR!
I'LL BE HERE!
THANK YOU SIR!

OH BOY OH BOY OH BOY OH BOY!
* SIGH * BEGGARS CAN'T BE CHOOSERS.

JUST WAIT 'TIL I CALL MY MOTHER AND TELL HER! SHE WON'T BELIEVE IT!

HELLO, MOTHER? GUESS WHAT!? I GOT A JOB!
OH? THAT'S NICE SON.

I BET YOU DIDN'T THINK I COULD DO IT, DIDJA!? HUH?! DIDJA?!
NOW, NOW, JUNIOR. ANYONE CAN GET A JOB...

WHAT'S IMPORTANT IS THAT YOU ENJOY YOUR WORK, AND...
OF COURSE I'LL ENJOY IT! IT'S AT AN ICE CREAM PARLOR, AND I LOVE ICE CREAM!

YES, WELL, THEY'RE NOT PAYING YOU TO EAT IT, JUNIOR.
HUH? OH, UH... SO WHAT?! I KNEW THAT! SHEESH!

I JUST HOPE YOU CAN STICK WITH IT. YOU'RE ON YOUR OWN NOW, AND YOU'LL BE NEEDING THE MONEY...
HEY, DON'T YOU WORRY ABOUT ME!...

I KNOW HOW TO TAKE CARE OF MYSELF! IN FACT, YOU MAY NOT BE HEARING FROM ME FOR A LONG TIME!
HMMM... WEEL. SEE ABOUT THAT! GOOD LUCK, SON. * CLICK *

* SNAP! *
(UMBILICAL CORD)
CLICK!

THE NEXT DAY...
GOOD, YOU'RE JUST IN TIME FOR THE LUNCH RUSH.

YOU WON'T HAVE THE TIME TO LEARN EVERYTHING BEFORE THE CROWD ARRIVES, SO YOU'RE JUST GONNA HAVE TO PLAY IT BY EAR.

HEY! WHERE ARE YOU GOING?
I'M TAKING MY LUNCH BREAK. YOUR FELLOW EMPLOYEES WILL SHOW YOU THE ROPES.

JOEL, SHERRILL, EXPLAIN TO THIS NEW WORKER HIS BASIC DUTIES. I'LL BE BACK SHORTLY.
YES SIR, MR. NELSON!
(DICKWIPE!)
(CHECK OUT HIS "MEMBERS ONLY" JACKET! WHAT A DILDO!)
2 for 1

WHAT'S YOUR NAME KIDDO?
JUNIOR. W-WHAT AM I SUPPOSED TO DO?
DON'T SWEAT IT, JUNIOR! THIS JOB'S A SNAP!

...JUST ASK EACH CUSTUMER WHAT FLAVOR THEY WANT AND IF THEY WANT IT IN A CUP OR A CONE. ALL OUR CONES ARE UP HERE AND THERE'S ONLY 10 DIFFERENT KINDS SO YOU'LL LEARN 'EM ALL FAST. ALL THE ICE CREAM FLAVORS ARE LABELED 'CEPT FOR SOME AND YOU'LL LEARN 'EM ALL IN A FEW MONTHS. NOW AS FOR THE MILK SHAKES AND SODAS WE HAVE 18 DIFFERENT KINDS...
?

UH-OH, HERE COMES THE RUSH! YOU'RE ON YOUR OWN, JUNIOR!
ON MY OWN?
YEAH. WE'RE ON OUR LUNCH BREAK!

GIMME A DOUBLE SCOOP OF BANANA PISTACHIO!
GIMME THE EGGPLANT PARMESAN FLAVOR!
HEY! I WAS HERE FIRST!
I SAID I WANTED A DIET CAFFEINE-FREE COKE! WITH NUTRA-SWEET!!!
I'LL HAVE A CHOCOLATE CHOCOLATE-CHIP MOCHA COCOA ALMOND FUDGE SUNDAE, WITH CHOCOLATE SPRINKLES!
IS, LIKE, YOUR ICE CREAM, LIKE, ALL NATURAL? LIKE?
I'LL HAVE PINEAPPLE PIZZA FLAVOR!
LOOK AT THE CLOD SERVING US!
COULD YOU PLEASE NAME ME ALL THE FLAVORS? AGAIN?
I SAID I WANTED A WAFER CONE!
THIS IS A FAULTY ESTABLISHMENT!
SNORT!
HEH-HEH!
LISTEN PAL! I'VE BEEN WAITING TO ORDER FOR HALF AN HOUR, AND I'M SLOWLY STARTING TO GET PISSED-OFF!!!
LET 'IM HAVE IT!
WHAT'S YOUR NAME YOUNG MAN? I'M FILING A COMPLAINT!
THIS IS AN OUTRAGE!
CAN'T YOU GUYS HELP ME OUT? PLEASE!
SORRY. IT'S AGAINST THE RULES.
JUST GRIN AND BEAR IT, KIDDO. THE FIRST DAY'S ALWAYS THE ROUGHEST.
SMOKE
PEOPLE
THE BEST DRESSED WORST DRESSED FOR 1986
STRANGER IN A STRANGE LAND
WHAT'S THE REASON FOR THIS HOLD-UP?!
UH-OH! MR. NELSON'S BACK.
JUNIOR WAS SITTING DOWN ON THE JOB, SIR!
I WAS NOT! THEY WERE!
EXCUSE ME, ARE YOU THE MANAGER? WE HAVE A COMPLAINT!
THIS NEW EMPLOYEE OF YOURS REFUSED TO SERVE US! WE DEMAND THAT HE BE FIRED IMMEDIATELY!
HMMM... THIS IS SERIOUS...
PEOPLE
STRANGER IN A STRANGE LAND

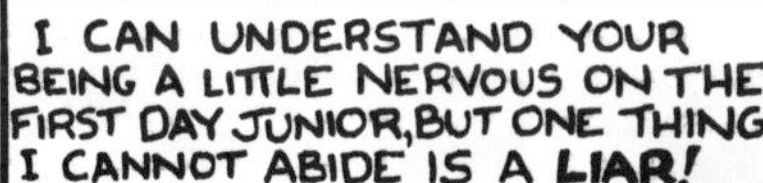

I CAN UNDERSTAND YOUR BEING A LITTLE NERVOUS ON THE FIRST DAY JUNIOR, BUT ONE THING I CANNOT ABIDE IS A LIAR!
BUT I'M NOT LYING! THEY ARE!

ALRIGHT JUNIOR, DON'T GO DIGGING YOURSELF INTO A DEEPER HOLE THAN YOU ALREADY ARE! I CAN SEE I'M GOING TO HAVE TO LEAN ON YOU PRETTY HEAVY IN ORDER TO HELP YOU GET OVER YOUR ATTITUDE PROBLEM.
"ATTITUDE PROBLEM"? "LEAN ON ME"?
YEAH!
← "MANAGER'S STANCE"

NORMALLY I WOULDN'T WASTE MY TIME LIKE THIS WITH A TROUBLESOME EMPLOYEE, BUT I SEE A LOT OF POTENTIAL IN YOU JUNIOR YOU COULD HAVE A GREAT CAREER AHEAD OF YOU IN FRANCHISED RESTAURANT MANAGEMENT.
"A CAREER IN FRANCHISED RESTAURANT MANAGEMENT"?

(THAT'S RIGHT, JUNIOR. YOU'RE IN FOR A GOOD BRAINWASHING!)
"BRAINWASHING"?!

ZOOM!
ZIP!
HEY!
?
?

THAT NIGHT...
...HELLO, MOTHER?...
RENT
END

JUNIOR

in "THE ROAD TO MANHOOD"

AND SO, FRANK PUTS JUNIOR TO WORK...

THAT NIGHT...

THIS WON'T DO... THIS WON'T DO AT ALL!

THE WAY THAT OLD SLAVE-DRIVER HAS ME GOING I'M GONNA DIE OF EXHAUSTION!

BUT THERE'S NOTHING I CAN DO ABOUT IT! I'M TRAPPED LIKE A RAT—A PRISONER IN MY OWN BOARDING HOUSE!

WELP, I GOT MYSELF INTO THIS MESS, SO I'VE GOT TO FIGURE A WAY TO GET MYSELF OUT!

MAYBE I'LL WIN THE LOTTERY!!!

...WHAT I REALLY NEED IS AN OPPORTUNITY TO PROVE MYSELF...

...SOMETHING CHALLENGING...SOMETHING THAT WILL SHOW EVERYONE THAT I CAN TAKE CARE OF MYSELF... THAT I'M NOT A SISSY...

I KNOW! I'LL LEARN TO DRIVE A CAR!!!

WHOA, LET'S NOT GET RECKLESS HERE! I OUGHTA AT LEAST LEARN HOW TO RIDE A BIKE FIRST!

PSSST! HEY JUNIOR! C'MERE!
?

YES, MR SILVERMAN?
HOW'D YOU LIKE TO EARN SOME EXTRA CASH BY DE-LIVERING A LETTER FOR ME?

GEE, I DON'T KNOW... I'M SUPPOSED TO BE WORKING FOR THE LANDLORD...
AAAH, DON'T WORRY ABOUT FRANK! I'LL CLEAR IT WITH HIM!

LOOK, ALL YOU GOTTA DO IS TAKE THIS ENVELOPE AND DROP IT OFF AT THIS DOWNTOWN ADDRESS...
DOWNTOWN!? I'VE NEVER BEEN DOWNTOWN BY MYSELF BEFORE! IT'S SCARY DOWN THERE!

WELL, IF YOU DON'T FEEL YOU'RE MAN ENOUGH FOR THE TASK...
I AM TOO MAN ENOUGH! GIMME THAT ENVELOPE!!

ATTABOY, JUNIOR! NOW WHEN YOU GET TO THIS PLACE, JUST DROP IT INTO THE MAIL-SLOT ON THE DOOR, AND THEN SPLIT!
IF ANYBODY ASKS ANY QUESTIONS SAY YOU DON'T KNOW ANYTHING: ACT DUMB.
THAT SOUNDS EASY.

YOU KNOW IT'S EASY! —HERE'S A TWENTY FOR YA, KIDDO. MAYBE YOU CAN GET YERSELF A PIECE OF ASS WHILE YOU'RE DOWN THERE! HEH HEH HEH...
A PIECE OF AN ASS?

DOWNTOWN...
HERE'S THE BUILDING...
176

414
...AND HERE'S THE ROOM, AND HERE'S THE MAIL SLOT! THAT WAS EASY ENOUGH!
MAIL

NOW I'LL JUST HEAD HOME AND...
HEY YOU! COME BACK HERE!
414
MAIL

WHO, ME?
YEAH, YOU! WE DON'T LIKE STRANGERS DROPPING THINGS OFF WITHOUT ANY EXPLANA-TIONS. YOU DIG ME?

YES, I CAN UNDERSTAND THAT...
GOOD! THEN YOU WON'T MIND WAITING HERE WHILE WE EXAMINE THE CONTENTS, AND MAYBE ASK A FEW QUESTIONS...
HEY, IT'S FROM THAT DEADBEAT SILVERMAN!

OH YEAH? MAYBE HE'S FINALLY PAYING BACK THAT TEN GRAND HE OWES US!
EXCEPT THERE'S ONLY TWO THOUSAND IN HERE... AND AN I.O.U!

WHAT?!? THAT SLIMEBALL KNOWS WE DON'T ACCEPT I.O.U'S!
HEY KID, DO YOU KNOW THIS SILVERMAN GUY?
SURE— I MEAN NO! I DON'T!!

WHICH IS IT, PUNK! YES OR NO?!?
YEEOWCH! I BEAN YETH! I DO KNOW HIMB! OOCH! OWCH! THE PAIN!
TWIST!
SQUEEZE!

GOOD! THEN PERHAPS YOU COULD TELL US WHERE WE MIGHT FIND HIM?
FIND HIM? ER...I... ...UH...

...LOOKS LIKE I'LL HAVE TO REFRESH HIS MEMORY AGAIN...
8425 166th AVENUE, ROOM NUMBER 4!!!

THANKS KID! YOU CAN GO NOW!
YEAH, WE WERE JUST THINKING OF PAYING OL' LARRY A VISIT, IS ALL! HEH HEH HEH...
HEY EDDIE, STRAIGHTEN OUT YOUR TOUPÉ, WILL YA?
...FER CRYIN' OUT LOUD.

LATER...

HOW'D IT GO, JUNIOR? PIECE OF CAKE, RIGHT?
WELL...

I DID WIND UP TALKING TO TWO FELLOWS WHO ASKED FOR YOUR ADDRESS...THEY SAID THEY'RE GOING TO PAY YOU A VISIT...
THEY WHAT!!?!

OH MY GOD! THEY'RE HERE!
KNOCK! KNOCK!!
YO' SILVERMAN!
OPEN UP!

THERE HE GOES — UP THE STAIRS!!
BASH!
?!

WHAT'S GOING ON?!
MR. SILVERMAN IS ENTERTAINING SOME OF HIS FRIENDS FROM DOWNTOWN.
SLAM! BAM! OPEN UP! BOOM! HALP!

GOOD LORD! THEY'RE GONNA KILL HIM! C'MON!
WHERE ARE WE GOING?

WE'VE GOTTA HIDE! IF THEY FIND US WE'RE DEAD TOO!
THOSE GUYS MEAN BUSINESS!

I CAN'T SEE! WHERE ARE WE?
WE'RE IN MY SECRET BASEMENT HIDEOUT!
NOW SIT STILL AND SHUT-UP!

I'M SCARED! DO YOU REALLY THINK THEY'LL KILL HIM?
ARE YOU KIDDING? JUST LISTEN TO 'EM UP THERE!
SMASH! CRASH! AAAH! NO! DON'T!

MAN OH MAN, IT SOUNDS LIKE OL' SILVERMAN HAS REALLY BOUGHT IT THIS TIME! OH WELL, HE WAS GONNA HAVE TO PAY FOR HIS SHENANIGANS SOONER OR LATER. IT WAS JUST A MATTER OF TIME...
BANG! BOOM!

AND WHAT'S THE BIG IDEA OF NOSING THROUGH MY PRIVATE STASH!?! HERE I AM TRYING TO SAVE YOUR LIFE AND YOU REPAY ME BY BARFING ALL OVER MY "SCIENCE" MAGAZINES"!!

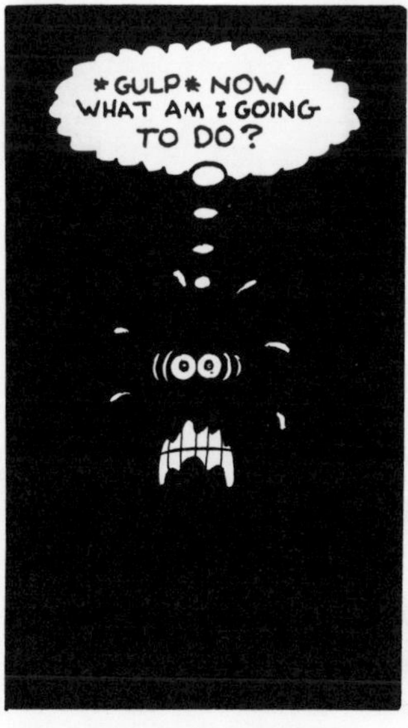

I'LL JUST CASUALLY WALK TO MY ROOM... WHAT'S THE BIG DEAL? THERE'S NO ONE HERE...
..ALIVE, THAT IS!

...SO FAR SO GOOD...

JUNIOR....

YIKES!!
...YEAH, I GOT PRETTY BEAT UP...LISTEN KID, YOU GOTTA HELP ME OUT...

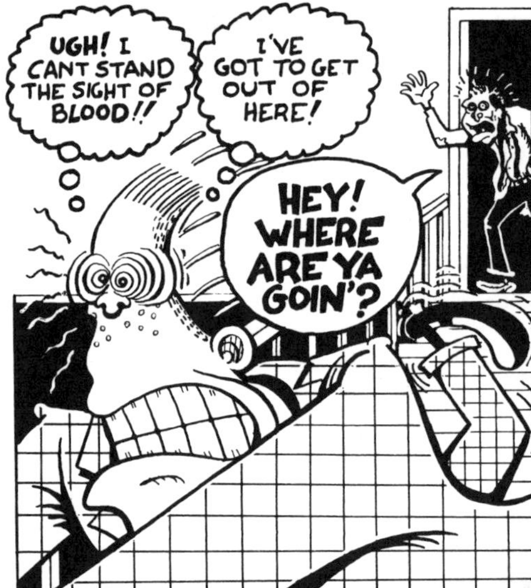
UGH! I CAN'T STAND THE SIGHT OF BLOOD!!
I'VE GOT TO GET OUT OF HERE!
HEY! WHERE ARE YA GOIN'?

SLAM!
...AAH, FUCK YEW, YA MISERABLE PIECE OF SHIT... GODDAM COWARD... ...FUCK..

LATER THAT NIGHT...
WHAT'S THAT NOISE?!
CRACKLE
SNAP

POP! CRACKLE!

SNAP! SNAP!

OH—IT'S YOU.
RIDE A RAINBOW!
SORRY I WOKE YOU, MOM. I WAS JUST HAVING MYSELF A BOWL OF RICE KRISPIES.
SNAP! CRACKLE! POP

SO, AM I TO ASSUME YOU'RE LIVING HERE AGAIN?
WELL, YOU KNOW, I'VE BEEN, WORRIED ABOUT YOU LATELY MOM, WHAT WITH NO MAN AROUND THE HOUSE AND ALL. FOR ALL YOU KNEW I COULDA BEEN A BURGLER!

JUNIOR, DO YOU REALLY THINK THAT BY COMING BACK HOME EVERYTHING WILL BE EXACTLY THE WAY THEY USED TO BE BEFORE YOU LEFT HOME?
WELL...WHY NOT? THERE'S NO REASON WHY THINGS CAN'T BE THE WAY THEY USED TO BE, IS THERE? HUH? IS THERE?
JM

* SIGH * WE'LL TALK ABOUT IT IN THE MORNING. GOOD NIGHT, SON.
G'NITE MOM, AND WOULD YOU LEAVE THE LIGHT ON? THANKS.

CRUNCH!

THESE RICE KRISPIES SURE TASTE GOOD!
END.

WHAT, ME NOT WORRY?

Junior in

© 1986 BY PETER BAGGE.

REASONS TO NEVER LEAVE YOUR HOUSE!

ANSWER ME THIS:
WHY WOULD ANYONE IN THEIR RIGHT MIND WANT TO LEAVE THE WARMTH AND SECURITY OF THEIR OWN HOME FOR A SINGLE MOMENT, ESPECIALLY IF THEY DON'T HAVE TO?

CHARLOTTE'S WEB

HOT COCOA

THE TRUTH IS THAT MOST PEOPLE LOOK DOWN THEIR NOSES AT ANYONE THAT STAYS HOME ALL THE TIME.

THEY CLAIM YOU CAN'T ENJOY LIFE TO THE FULLEST UNLESS YOU GET OUT AND ABOUT!

BUT I DON'T ASSOCIATE GOING OUT WITH "LIVING", I ASSOCIATE IT WITH FEAR, DANGER AND DEATH!

LET'S FACE IT — IT'S A DANGEROUS WORLD OUT THERE!!!

ANYTHING CAN HAPPEN TO YOU IN THE OUTSIDE WORLD—THINGS THAT YOU HAVE ABSOLUTELY NO CONTROL OVER! LIKE...
...GETTING HIT BY A TRUCK...
BASH!

...OR BY LIGHTNING...
ZAP!

...OR BY A FALLING TREE...
SPLAT!

...OR BY A FALLING ASTEROID!
SQUASH!

OR YOU COULD VERY LIKELY BE HARASSED OR MUGGED OR KIDNAPPED OR MURDERED OR WORSE!
PLEASE JOIN OUR CHURCH!
IN FACT WE INSIST!

BONK!

FLUMP!

BANG!
STAB!

THE STREETS AND BUILDINGS ARE FULL OF PEOPLE WHO ARE A LOT SMARTER, STRONGER, BIGGER, QUICKER, MEANER, RICHER, CRAZIER, BETTER EDUCATED AND MORE AMBITIOUS THAN YOU'LL EVER BE, AND THEY'RE ALL OUT TO TAKE ADVANTAGE OF YOU AND MAKE YOUR LIFE AS MISERABLE AS POSSIBLE! YOU HAVEN'T GOT A CHANCE!
...YES SIR, THE OUTSIDE WORLD IS TO BE AVOIDED AT ALL COSTS!

OF COURSE I'M AWARE OF THE FACT THAT MOST ACCIDENTS OCCUR IN THE HOME, BUT THESE ARE USUALLY THE RESULT OF PEOPLE WORKING WITH HEAVY MACHINERY OR FROM JUST DOING ODD JOBS AROUND THE HOUSE.
THESE ACCIDENTS CAN EASILY BE AVOIDED BY SIMPLY NOT DOING ANY HOUSEHOLD CHORES OR REPAIRS!
AFTER ALL, WHAT COULD POSSIBLY HAPPEN TO YOU IF YOU JUST STAYED IN BED OR IN YOUR EASY CHAIR ALL DAY?
SLICE!
FALL...
CRACK!
BZZZZZT!

I ALSO REALIZE THAT THE OUTSIDE WORLD CAN ALWAYS INTRUDE UPON YOUR HOME IN THE FORMS OF BURGLARS, ARSONISTS, SALESMEN, ETC...

ALL I CAN SUGGEST IS TO PROTECT YOURSELF TO THE GREATEST EXTENT POSSIBLE BY INVESTING IN FIRE AND BURGLAR ALARMS, CYCLONE FENCES, WATCHDOGS AND FLOODLIGHTS.
THIS IS THE ONE AREA WHERE I FEEL THAT YOU AND YOUR FAMILY SHOULD SPARE NO EXPENSE!

I ALSO SUGGEST THAT YOU NEVER, EVER ANSWER YOUR DOOR IF YOU'RE NOT EXPECTING ANY GUESTS.
DING! DONG!
AVON CALLING!
FINE YOUNG MAN BRUTALLY TORTURED AND MURDERED BY BOGUS AVON LADY

NOW, I KNOW THERE ARE MANY OF YOU WHO HAVE TO LEAVE YOUR HOUSE EVEN THOUGH YOU DON'T WANT TO, LIKE TO GET TO A JOB OR TO SHOP FOR YOUR GROCERIES. YET THESE TOO CAN BE AVOIDED IF YOU PUT YOUR MIND TO IT!
TAP! TAP!

THE SIMPLEST WAY FOR A PERSON TO ENJOY A RECLUSIVE LIFESTYLE LIKE MINE IS TO LIVE WITH AND OFF OF YOUR RELATIVES!
IT'S EASY TO MAKE A SYMPATHETIC AND UNDERSTANDING PARENT OR GUARDIAN — LIKE MY MOTHER — REALIZE THAT IT'S JUST PLAIN OL' IMPOSSIBLE FOR A YOUNG PERSON TO FIND A DECENT JOB OR APARTMENT THESE DAYS!
IF YOU CAN MANAGE TO AVOID GETTING ON THEIR NERVES AS THE YEARS GO BY, YOU'LL WIND UP INHERITING THE WHOLE SHE-BANG ONCE THEY KICK OFF!

OF COURSE YOU MAY NOT HAVE A NICE UNDERSTANDING FAMILY LIKE I DO, AND THAT MAKES THINGS A BIT TOUGHER, BUT THERE ARE STILL WAYS FOR YOU TO AFFORD TO LIVE THE "SAFE LIFE" — YOU JUST HAVE TO LOOK FOR 'EM!
LIKE TAKE A LOOK AT THIS...

...WHY, THIS PUBLICATION IS CHOCK FULL OF ADS FOR EASY, WORK-AT-HOME SCHEMES! THIS AD HERE SAYS THAT BY STUFFING ENVELOPES AT HOME YOU COULD POTENTIALLY EARN HUGE PROFITS!
ISN'T THAT GREAT?!
EARN BIG CA$H!
HERE'S HOW:

OR YOU COULD ALWAYS ROB A BANK OR COMMIT SOME OTHER MAJOR CRIME! I ADMIT THERE'S A CONSIDERABLE AMOUNT OF RISK INVOLVED IN AN UNDERTAKING LIKE THAT, BUT IF YOU PULL IT OFF AND GET AWAY WITH IT, YOU'LL BE ON EASY STREET!

SO DO WHAT I DO: WHEN THEY ARRIVE AT YOUR DOOR, HAVE THEM SLIP THE BILL THROUGH THE MAIL SLOT, EXAMINE IT CAREFULLY, THEN SLIP THEM THE MONEY THE SAME WAY. HAVE THEM LEAVE THE PACKAGE(S) ON THE DOOR STEP BUT **DO NOT** OPEN THE DOOR UNTIL YOU ARE COMPLETELY SURE THEY'RE GONE!

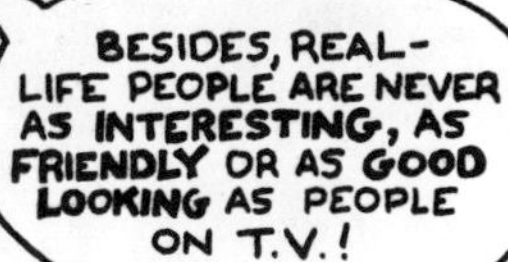

AH YES, A MAN'S HOME IS HIS CASTLE! TRUER WORDS WERE NEVER SPOKEN!
EVERYTHING IS ARRANGED JUST THE WAY YOU WANT IT! EVERY OBJECT IS SO FAMILIAR, SO FULL OF MEMORIES, SO MUCH A PART OF YOU! HOW COULD ANYONE BEAR TO PART WITH ALL OF THIS FOR A SINGLE SECOND?
HAPPY BIRTHDAY!
Photos
YOU'RE A GOOD MAN, CHARLIE BROWN!
WORLDS FAIR
B
ONLY WHEN YOU'RE AT HOME BY YOURSELF CAN YOU PLAY YOUR FAVORITE RECORDS, READ YOUR FAVORITE BOOKS AND WATCH YOUR FAVORITE T.V. SHOWS AND MOVIES ANY TIME YOUR LITTLE HEART DESIRES!
...WOOPS THERE GOES ANOTHER RUBBER TREE PLANT!
FORGET ABOUT TRAVELLING! WHEN YOU'VE SEEN ONE CITY OR MOUNTAIN OR SEASHORE OR SUNSET YOU'VE SEEN 'EM ALL! BESIDES, ALL THESE PLACES ALWAYS LOOK NICER IN THE TRAVEL ADS IN MAGAZINES ANYWAY.
VISIT HAWAII
TRAVEL WORLD

THE SAME GOES FOR PARADES, CONCERTS AND SPORTING EVENTS! WHO WANTS TO BE PUSHED, JOSTLED AND SHOVED AROUND, NOT TO MENTION RIPPED-OFF, WHAT WITH THE OUTRAGEOUS PRICES THEY CHARGE FOR TICKETS, FOOD AND PARKING THESE DAYS!

NO SIR, I CAN ENJOY ALL OF THOSE THINGS RIGHT HERE IN THE PRIVACY OF MY OWN HOME!
DRIP!

HEY, WHAT'S THIS? COULD IT BE?...
DRIP!
DROP!

OH NO! THE ROOF IS LEAKING! MOTHER! MOTHER COME QUICK!

DARN, I FORGOT, SHE ISN'T HOME! TYPICAL OF HER! NOW I'LL HAVE TO CALL A REPAIR MAN...

HELLO, ACME ROOFING? THIS IS AN EMERGENCY! MY ROOF IS LEAKING AND I...

WHAT?!? SINCE WHEN DON'T YOU WORK ON GROUND HOG DAY!? WHAT AM I SUPPOSED TO DO NOW!?!...

FIX IT MYSELF!?! ARE YOU KIDDING? I COULD GET KILLED! NOW SEE HERE, I'M GETTING ALL WET AND I'M LIABLE TO CATCH PNEUMONIA AND I...
...AND... I ... UH-OH...
CRACK!

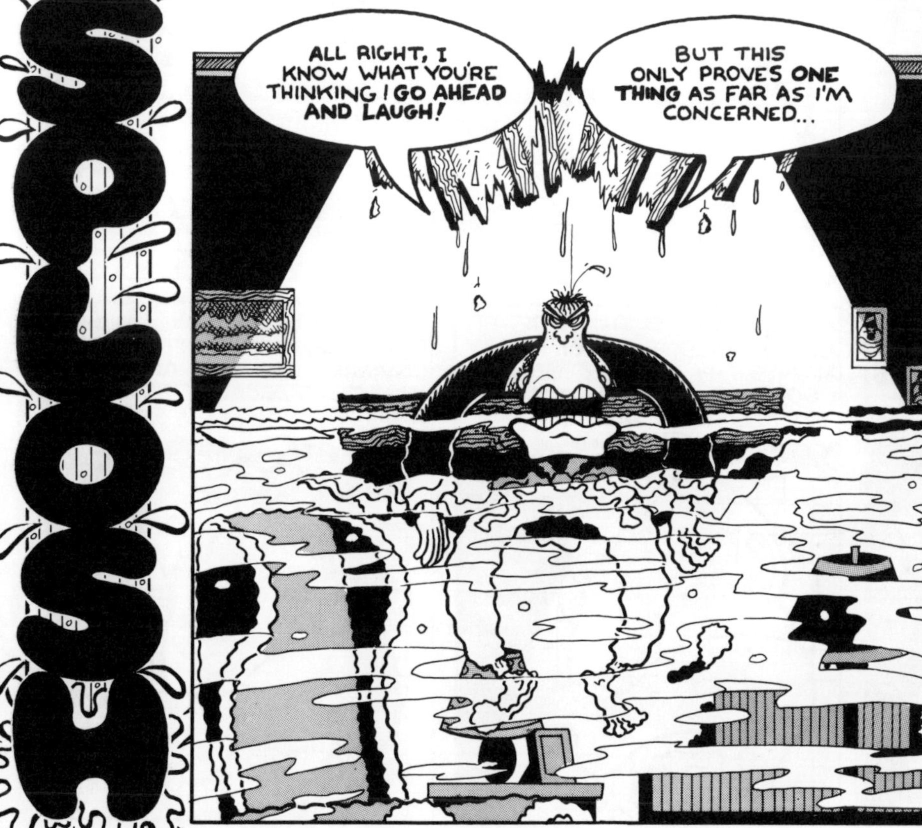

SOS
ALL RIGHT, I KNOW WHAT YOU'RE THINKING! GO AHEAD AND LAUGH!
BUT THIS ONLY PROVES ONE THING AS FAR AS I'M CONCERNED...

LIFE IS NOT PERFECT!
END.

SIGH WHAT AN EMPTY LIFE I LEAD...THERE'S SIMPLY NOTHING TO IT... NO EXCITEMENT...NO RAZZAMATAZZ...

I OUGHT TO GET OUT AND ABOUT MORE OFTEN. MEET NEW PEOPLE! EXPERIENCE NEW EXPERIENCES! I OUGHTA START LIVING A LIFE RIGHT TODAY!...

NO, WAIT, DOLLY'S ON TONIGHT...

♫ "...DUM DA DE... A COAT MADE OF PATCHES..."♫ ...I LOVE THAT SONG...IT'S ONE OF MY ALL-TIME FAVORITE SONGS, I'D SAY...

HEY, I SHOULD TRY WRITING A SONG! I'M THE SENSITIVE TYPE! ...BUT WHAT SHOULD I WRITE ABOUT?...I KNOW, I'LL WRITE A SONG ABOUT A FAITHFUL DOG!

NAH, FORGET IT. I'VE NEVER EVEN HAD A DOG. IN FACT I HATE DOGS! SO CAN THAT IDEA...

I WONDER WHY I HATE DOGS SO MUCH...MAYBE IT'S BECAUSE DOGS HATE ME... THOUGH CATS HATE ME TOO, AND I LIKE CATS...

GOSH, COME TO THINK OF IT, ALL ANIMALS HATE ME! THEY ALWAYS TRY TO BITE ME WHEN I GO NEAR THEM! BUT THEN SO DO MOST HUMANS!...

I DON'T KNOW WHY I'M SO DISLIKED, WHAT WITH MY CHARMING RED HAIR AND ALL... MAYBE IT'S BECAUSE I'M SUCH A SISSY...YEAH, I GUESS THAT'S IT...

BUT GEE WHIZ, SISSIES NEED LOVE TOO!

...I CANT HELP IT IF I'M SUCH A WIMP! IT'S NOT MY FAULT I TURNED OUT THIS WAY...

...IT'S MY MOTHER'S FAULT!

SHE MADE ME THE WAY I AM, NO QUESTION ABOUT IT! AND SHE DID IT ON PURPOSE TOO, THAT CALCULATING WITCH!...

ALL HER TALK ABOUT WISH-ING I WOULD MOVE OUT ON MY OWN IS JUST THAT— TALK! SHE ACTUALLY COULDN'T BEAR IT IF I LEFT AND SHE KNOWS IT!

SHE'S MADE ME A PRISONER OF MY OWN PERSONALITY! I'M AN EMOTIONAL CRIPPLE THANKS TO HER!! I'M A VICTIM OF CHILD ABUSE!

I THINK IT'S ABOUT TIME I CONFRONT HER WITH HER CRIMES! WE NEED TO HASH THIS THING OUT FACE-TO-FACE!

...BUT WAIT, MAYBE I'M BEING TOO HASTY IN MY ACCUSA-TIONS...SHE PROBABLY DIDN'T MEAN TO BE A LOUSY MOTHER ...BUT THERE STILL IS ONE THING I'LL HAVE TO DISCUSS WITH HER, AND THAT IS...

...SHE FORGOT TO BUY TOILET PAPER AGAIN!
END

JUNIOR

JUNIOR
RRR-IPP!

CRACKLE!
CRUNCH!

TOSS!

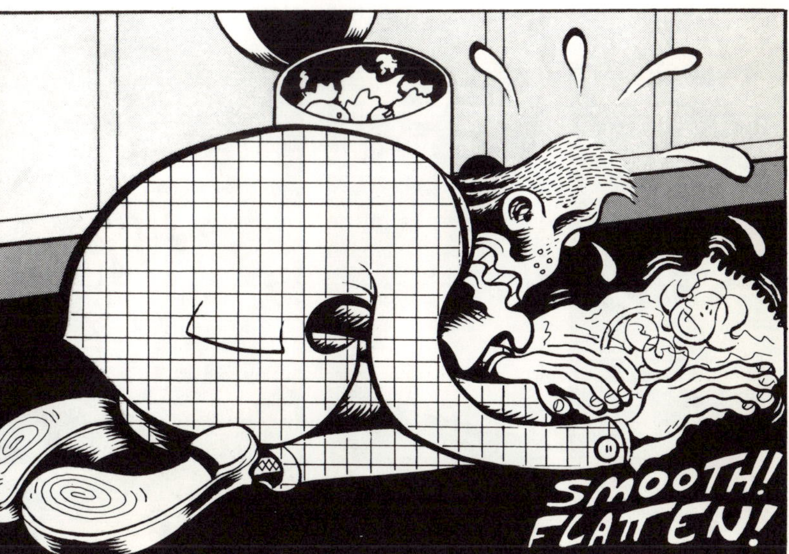

SMOOTH!
FLATTEN!

JUNIOR
HANG IN THERE, BABY
THE GLORY OF NATURE

CLICK!

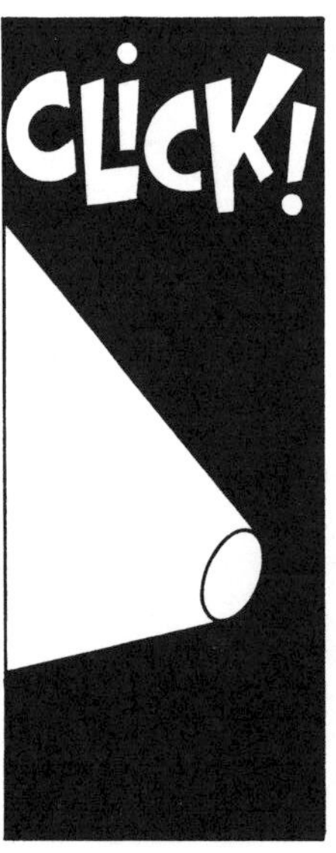
CLICK!

© '89 P. BAGGE

RIP! TEAR!
SHRED!

©'89 P. BAGGE

JUNIOR
6:30 PM
MILK
MAPLE SYRUP

DING!
DONG!
7:00 PM
MILK

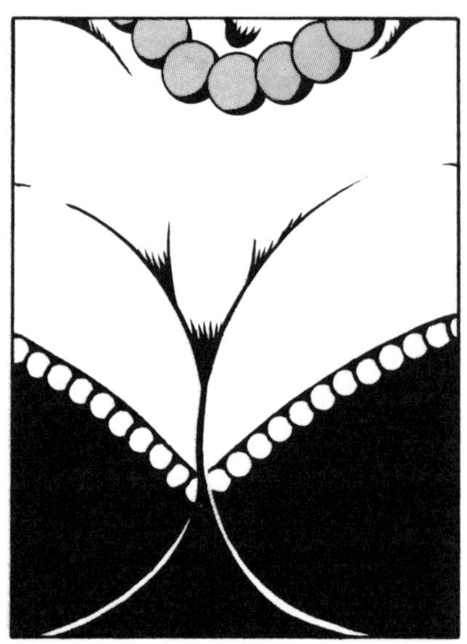

© '89 P. BAGGE

PUBLIC
LIBRARY

GE
LY
99
THE
NE
HUMAN
SEXUAL
700-79
SOCIOL

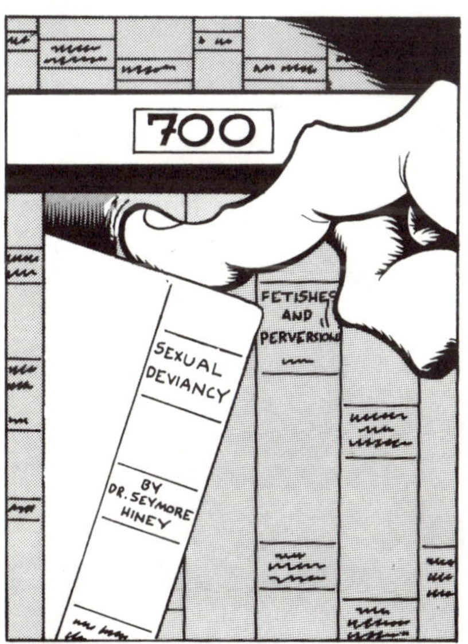

700
SEXUAL
DEVIANCY
BY
DR. SEYMORE
HINEY
FETISHES
AND
PERVERSION

Excessive masturbation
coupled with objectification
of specific image bearing rese
of specific image bearing rese
implies arrested development or
post-pubescent male blah blah blah...
emphasis on female breasts, suggests
oedipus complex blah blah.... sexual rep
obsession of mother or maternal
figure...possessive behavior tow
highly repressed sexual express
blah, blah, blah...of a specif
type lacking social skill
yadda yadda...
highly fucked up
etc, etc, ad
nauseum

JUNIOR

RIP! TEAR!
SHRED!

PORN
REAL ART!

THE NEXT DAY...

?
!

© '89 P. BAGGE

© '89 P. BAGGE

JUNIOR

JUNIOR IS A PORNOGRAPHER
SEXUAL DEVIANT
I AM A MASTURBATOR
PERVERT

HERE LIES JUNIOR
"IT WAS THE ONLY HONORABLE THING TO DO"

SNAP!

HAWLP!

BZZZT!

© '89 P. BAGGE

JUNIOR
?

?

!
THE FANCY PANTS,
HIGH—FALLOOTIN'
ART GALLERY
DATE: MAY
Pay to the Order of JUNIOR
ONE MILLION DOLL
ADVANCE

= $

THE NEXT DAY...

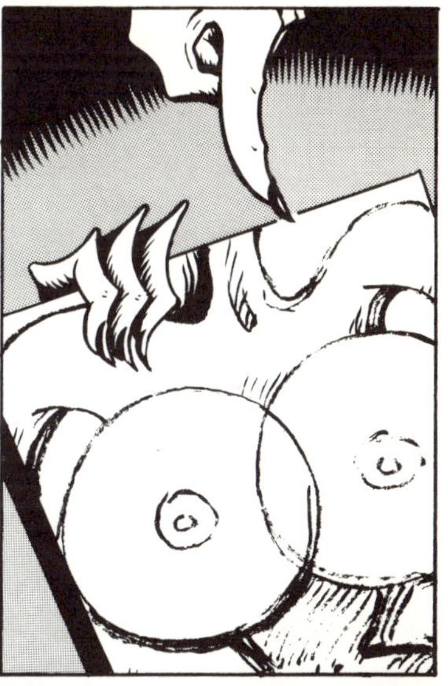

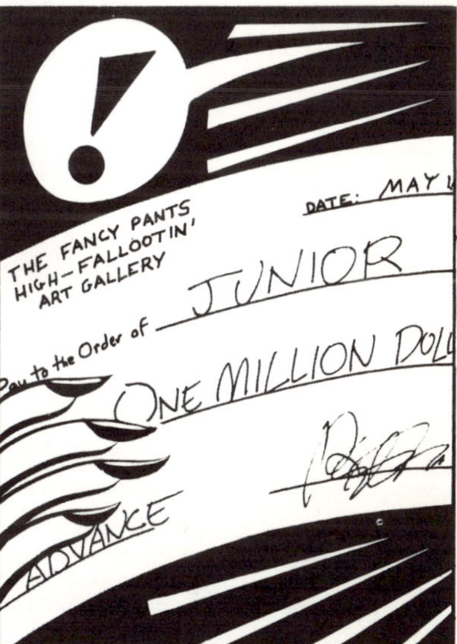

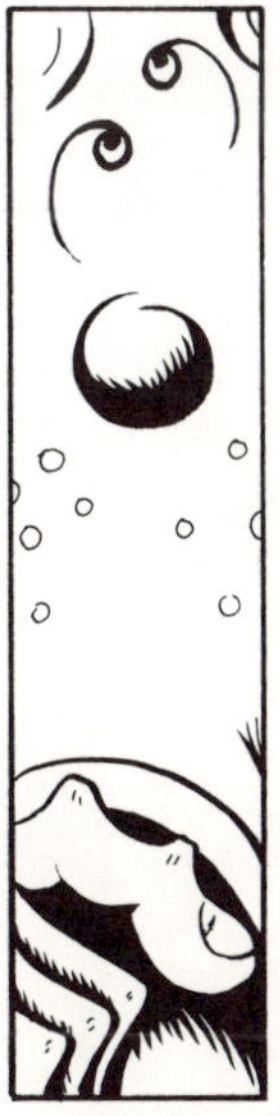

©'89 P. BAGGE

CHET AND BUNNY LEEWAY

"A CYNIC'S WORK IS NEVER DONE."

Y'KNOW, THIS IS A WACKY WORLD WE LIVE IN!
HOW DO YOU FIGURE?

WELL, LIKE SOMETIMES YOU THINK IT'S MONDAY WHEN IT'S ACTUALLY TUESDAY!
I SEE...

YOU MEAN LIKE WHEN YOU THINK THAT YOU'RE EATING BREAKFAST BUT IT TURNS OUT THAT YOU'RE EATING YOUR LUNCH!
EXACTLY!

THAT REMINDS ME OF THE TIME I THOUGHT I WAS EATING ROAST HAM BUT IT TURNED OUT I WAS EATING MY RIGHT ARM!
THAT WAS SO EMBARRASSING!

THAT HAPPENED ON OUR FIRST DATE, DIDN'T IT?
YES, WE WERE GOING TO SEE "ENDLESS LOVE" BUT WOUND UP GOING TO A TATTOO PARLOR.

I REMEMBER YOU WANTING TO POKE ME IN THE TIT WITH A FORK, BUT I SAID "NEVER ON A FIRST DATE"!
BUT ON OUR SECOND DATE WE "FORKED" LIKE CRAZY! HA-HA!

YOU KNOW, SOMETIMES YOU'RE A SWELL GUY, AND OTHER TIMES YOU'RE A REAL JACKASS!
WHICH AM I NOW?
OH YEAH? WELL SOMETIMES YOU LOOK LIKE A REAL FOX, AND OTHER TIMES YOU LOOK LIKE A DOG!
PIG!!
TRY THIS GAME AT HOME.
WE SURE DO TEAR EACH OTHER APART SOMETIMES!
YEAH, BUT WE ALWAYS GET BACK TOGETHER.
"PATCHING UP OUR RELATIONSHIP" CAN USE UP ALOT OF CRAZY GLUE!
I'M STILL MISSING SOME VERTEBRAS, AND I'M HOLDING YOU RESPONSIBLE!
Y'KNOW, WE GO THROUGH THIS SAME NONSENSE EVERY SINGLE DAY!
YOU'RE RIGHT...
PLOP!
KLUNK!
I GUESS IT ISN'T SUCH A WACKY WORLD AFTER ALL.
©1983 BY PETER BAGGE

I HAVEN'T PLAYED MY OLD SINGLES COLLECTION IN AGES!
THIS IS GOING TO BE FUN!
TRUCK! TRUCK!

DO IT ANY WAY, YA WANNA, DO IT, DOITANYWAYYAWANNA...
TAP! TAP!

HEY! YA PLAYIN' OLD REKKIDS?!
YUP!
...I'M TALKIN' SQUARE BIZ TO YA BAY-BUH, SQUARE, SQUARE BIZ...

OOH! I USED TO LOVE THIS SONG!
...ROCK THE BOAT—DON'T ROCK THE BOAT BAYBUH,— ROCK THE BOAT...
SHIMMY! SHIMMY!

I WISH YOU WOULDN'T DANCE. YOU'RE MAKING THE TURNTABLE WOBBLE.
OH PHOOEY ON YOU!
...I WANT TO TAKE YOU- DANGADANK!- FUNKYTOWN!
TWIST! TWIST!

I DON'T SEE HOW YOU CAN JUST SIT THERE AND NOT DANCE TO IT. IT'S GOT SUCH A GREAT BEAT!
BECAUSE I DON'T LIKE TO MAKE A FOOL OF MYSELF IS WHY!
DO IT 'TIL YOUR SATISFIED...
GYRATE! GYRATE!

...HMM HMM MM...SUPER FREAK, THE GIRL'S A SUPER FREAK, YOW! YOW!!...
OH NO! PLEASE DON'T SING!
...SUPER FREAK... ...SUPER FREAK

HEY, IF YOU CAN DANCE TO THE RECORDS THEN I CAN SING TO THEM!
BUT YOU'VE GOT SUCH A HORRIBLE SINGING VOICE.
...SHE'S A SUPER FREAK! YOW!

IZZAT SO?! WELL THAT'S TOO BAD!...
SUPER FREAK! THE GIRL'S A SUPER FREAK! YOW! YOW!!
OKAY, BE THAT WAY!

OARAAKKK! BLLAAKK!!
TO THE "TUNE" OF "SUPER-FREAK"
OH NO! NOT THE TRUMPET!

TIT FOR TAT, WISE GUY!
OH, SO THAT'S THE WAY IT IS, HUH?! WE'LL SEE ABOUT THAT...
BLLACKLLK!
BRAPP!
BLAPP!
SQUAWKK!
CRACKK!

YIKES! NOT THE MARSHALL AMP!
I'VE GOT IT CRANKED UP TO "10"! HA! HA! HA!
Marshall
Marshall
BLANNG!

– CLICK! –
HEY! WHA HOPPEN?!

YOU BLEW A FUSE, YOU PEA BRAIN!
OH.

...SUPER FREAK...
DON'T SING!

THE END.

LIFE'S A BITCH AND THEN YOU DIE!

SO WHAT ARE YOU GOING TO DO ON YOUR GLORIOUS DAY OFF?
I'M THINKING I MIGHT SPEND THE AFTERNOON AT THE MALL.

THE MALL?!? YOU ALWAYS GET SO CRANKY AND DEPRESSED WHENEVER YOU GO TO THAT PLACE!
THAT'S BECAUSE THE ONLY TIME WE EVER GO IS WHEN WE'RE CHRISTMAS SHOPPING OR WHEN YOU DRAG ME TO BUY NEW CLOTHES!
I HATE DOING THAT STUFF!

THIS TIME I'M JUST GONNA BUM AROUND, WASTE MONEY AND HAVE A TOTALLY UNCONSTRUCTIVE DAY!
SOUNDS SWELL, BUT DON'T WASTE TOO MUCH MONEY, AND REMEMBER TO DRIVE SAFE!

WHADAYA MEAN?! I ALWAYS DRIVE SAFE!
YOU DRIVE LIKE A MADMAN, ESPECIALLY WHEN YOU'RE CRANKY.
...NOW EXCUSE ME WHILE I GET READY FOR THE SALT MINES...
WALK OF THE DAMNED!
TRUDGE TRUDGE

THE NERVE OF THAT WOMAN, TALKING TO ME LIKE I'M SOME IRRESPONSIBLE TEENAGER! "DRIVE LIKE A MADMAN"— INDEED!
C'MON! MOVE IT, GRAMPS! GET THE LEAD OUT!
BEEP! HONK! BEEP! HONK!
?

...NOW LET'S SEE, WHICH MALL SHALL I GO TO: THE OLD, RUN-DOWN BUT CHEAP MALL, OR THE NEW GLITZY BUT EXPENSIVE MALL?...
HEY, BACK OFF, PAL! WE AIN'T PLAYIN' FOLLOW THE LEADER!
?
HONK!! BEEP! HONK! BEEP!
BEEP! HONK! BEEP!
HONK
BEEP! BEEP!

THERE IS A LOT OF HOUSEHOLD STUFF WE COULD USE THAT I COULD PICK UP AT THE OLD MALL FOR REALLY CHEAP...
THEN AGAIN, THAT PLACE IS FULL OF WELFARE MOTHERS AND THEIR SCREAMING KIDS, WHILE THE "SCENERY" AT THE NEW MALL IS MUCH NICER...

AW HECK, IT'S NO CONTEST! I'M OPTING FOR THE GLITZ!
MALL BABES HERE I COME!
VARROOM!

AT THE MALL...
VIDEOV
VIDEOVILLE!
WORLD'S LARGEST SELECTION
GRAND OPENING CELEBRATION!
MOE'S MEATS
YES! WE HAVE WHOLE-GRAIN LIVERWURST $3.98 lb.
WOW! LOOK AT THIS VIDEO STORE! "WORLD'S LARGEST SELECTION", I'VE GOTTA CHECK THIS OUT!

HEY, THEY DO HAVE A GOOD SELECTION HERE!
LOOK AT ALL THESE OLD MOVIES! YOU CAN'T FIND THESE ANYWHERE!
WESTERNS A-Z
MYSTERIES A-Z
MUSICALS A-Z
COMEDY A-Z

LET US GO IN HERE, DARLEEN!
OH RAD, A VIDEO STORE! WAY COOL!
SHEESH! GET A LOAD OF THAT LATIN-LOVER TYPE IN THE WHITE JUMP SUIT AND HIS BRAT-FACED GIRL-FRIEND!

YOU DO HAVE AN IMPRESSIVE SELECTION HERE, BUT WHO CARES ABOUT ALL THIS OLD STUFF? WHAT IS IMPORTANT IS BEING THE FIRST TO GET ALL THE NEW RELEASES. THAT IS THE SIGN OF A GOOD VIDEO STORE.
OH BROTHER! WILL YOU LISTEN TO THAT JERK!
YEAH, WELL, WE TRY.
HEY ALFONSE! LET'S RENT "E.T." AGAIN!
MANAGER
E.T.
JAWS

AH YES, THE GREAT STEVEN SPIELBERG! ONCE AGAIN HE WAS SNUBBED AT THE OSCARS. CLEARLY THE ACADEMY IS QUITE JEALOUS OF HIS SUPERIOR TALENTS.
GOOD GOD! NOW HE'S DEFENDING THE "GREATNESS" OF STEVEN SPIELBERG!
UH, YEAH, I GUESS.
UNTERS THIRD KIND
E.T
JAWS

OH NO! NOW SHE'S PRANCIN' AND SHOWIN' OFF ALL OVER THE STORE!
HEY ALFONSE! LOOKIT WHAT I LEARNED IN JAZZ DANCE CLASS TODAY!
WHAT IS IT ABOUT DANCERS THAT THEY GOTTA "PRACTICE" WHEREVER THEY GO?
LEAP!
TWIRL!
BOUNCE!

DARLEEN IS A PROFESSIONAL DANCER, YOU KNOW. I'M HER AGENT...
I'M GONNA BE IN AN UPCOMING DR. PEPPER COMMERCIAL. IT WON'T BE SHOWN HERE, THOUGH...
IT'LL SERVE AS GREAT EXPOSURE. WE EXPECT IT TO OPEN A LOT OF DOORS...
SHUT-UP YOU ASSHOLES!
HOW DARE YOU SPREAD YOUR ASS-HOLISHNESS ALL OVER MY NEW VIDEO STORE! GET OUT! GET OUT I SAY!!!

...BLAH BLAH BLAH DANCING...
...BLAH BLAH BLAH SPIELBERG...
...BLAH BLAH BLAH...
AW FERGET IT! I'M GETTIN' OUTTA HERE!
LDS LARGEST

THE MALL SURE LOOKS DESERTED TODAY... WHERE'S ALL THE CUTE LIL' HIGH SCHOOL GIRLS IN THEIR CUTE LIL' OUTFITS?
THEY'RE PROBABLY SLEEPING LATE AFTER A WILD NIGHT OF HEAVY PARTYING AND HARD DRUGS, THE POOR LIL' THINGS.
...UGH, LISTEN TO ME. I SOUND LIKE A DIRTY OLD MAN!
OH WELL, IF THE SHOE FITS...
PITCH IN!
SALE 50 OFF
FREE ITEMS!

PAY 'N' SAVE
HMMM... PAY 'N' SAVE IS HAVIN' A SALE ON ALL HOUSE- HOLD ITEMS...
MIGHT AS WELL BUY SOME CARPET CLEANER WHILE I'M HERE...
INCREDIBLE SAVINGS!
20% OFF ON ALL ITEMS!
ON SALE HANDI- WIPES!
ACME

LET'S SEE... WHAT OTHER STORE MIGHT I WANDER INTO....
NOTHING LOOKS VERY INTERESTING ALONG THIS CORRIDOR...
WOMEN'S APPAREL
Q-T BOUTIQUE
SHOE-FOR-MORE
ITALIAN IMPORTS FROM WALNUT VALLEY N.Y.

JEE-ZIZ! ALL THESE PLACES EITHER SELL CLOTHES AT OUTRAGEOUS PRICES OR WORTH- LESS GIFTS AT EVEN MORE OUTRAGEOUS PRICES!
THE APPAREL BARREL
CLOTHES FER-BRATS
THEY'RE HERE!
BUY
IMPORTED!!

WHY ARE THERE SO MANY OF THESE SILLY USELESS SHOPS!?!?
NUTTY STUFF!
THE SUNSHINE COUNTRY KITCHEN
THE ONE-STOP WHOLE-EARTH COOKIN' 'N' CRAFT SHOP!
JUST ARRIVED! HAND EMBROIDERED FOOTIE-WARMERS! (MADE IN ECUADOR) ONLY $39.95!!! COMES IN BUNNY OR KITTEN PATTERNS
INDIAN POTTERY!!

LOOK AT THIS! A WHOLE STORE THAT SELLS NOTHING BUT FUZZY-WUZZLES! WHAT THE HELL IS A "FUZZY-WUZZLE"? ONLY THE SILLIEST, CORNIEST PEOPLE MUST PAT- RONIZE AND OPERATE THESE STORES, YET THERE'S MILLIONS OF THEM!!!
THE FUZZY- WUZZLE SHOP
THEY WANT YOUR LOVE!
WE WANT YOUR MONEY!

HERE'S THAT FANCY DEPARTMENT STORE THE MRS. IS SO NUTS ABOUT...
...HEY, I KNOW! I'LL GO IN HERE AND BUY HER A PRESENT!
FREDERICK VON NORDSTROM AND COMPANY AND SONS DIRECTORY

SHE'LL BE SO SURPRISED! I TEND TO BE A BIT OF A CAD IN THE PRESENT- BUYING DEPARTMENT.
I'LL BUY HER A BOTTLE OF HER FAVORITE PERFUME!
UP

WHAT WAS THAT STUFF CALLED AGAIN? OH YEAH!...
...UH, HOW MUCH FOR A BOTTLE OF "ODE DU LA PAREÉ"?
FOR HER

IT DEPENDS, SIR. OUR SMALLEST BOTTLE GOES FOR $59.95.
FIFTY-NINE NINTEY-FIVE?! FOR THAT?!...OH, UH... UM, DO YOU HAVE A BANK MACHINE AROUND HERE?
FOR HER

CERTAINLY, SIR. GO RIGHT OUTSIDE THIS DOOR AND THEN TURN LEFT.
THANKS. I'LL BE RIGHT BACK!
FOR HER

I GOTTA REMAIN CALM UNTIL I GET OUTSIDE...
XXX

ONCE OUTSIDE...
ENTER
EXIT
SIXTY DOLLARS FOR THAT TEENY-TINY BOTTLE!?!
THAT COSTS MORE THAN HEROIN!!!

ENTER
EXIT
I CAN'T AFFORD TO SPEND THAT KIND OF MONEY ON AN EENTSY-WEENTSY BOTTLE OF PERFUME!
I'LL JUST HAVE TO GET HER SOMETHING ELSE.

ENTER
EXIT
WHO AM I KIDDING? I CAN'T GO BACK IN THERE. I'M SURE EVERYTHING IS A TOTAL RIP-OFF!
I DOUBT MY HEART COULD STAND THE STRAIN.

I MIGHT AS WELL HEAD HOME, IN TOTAL DEFEAT...
...AT LEAST MY REPUTATION AS A CAD REMAINS IN TACT.
MALL!
TO MULTI-LEVEL PARKING GARAGE →

I DON'T GET IT. HOW COULD ANYONE AFFORD TO SPEND SO MUCH MONEY ON SUCH NON-NECESSITIES?!
I KNOW THERE'S A LOT OF RICH PEOPLE IN THIS WORLD, BUT ARE THERE THAT MANY EVEN IN THIS ONE TOWN THAT CAN SUPPORT THIS ENTIRE MALL?!?
8-6
34

I SUPPOSE A "PROPER" HUSBAND IS EXPECTED TO SPEND MORE THAN HE CAN AFFORD ON HIS WIFE AND NOT MAKE A BIG STINK ABOUT IT. AT LEAST MY WIFE DOESN'T EXPECT ANYTHING LIKE THAT FROM ME...
...THEN AGAIN, SHE KNEW SHE DIDN'T HIT THE JACKPOT WHEN SHE MARRIED ME.
?!
X-3

I'M SUPRISED THEY EVEN ALLOW LOW-LIFES LIKE ME INTO THIS MALL! ALL I DO IS TAKE UP SPACE!
I BELONG IN THE DISCOUNT FLEA-MARKET MALL WITH ALL THE WELFARE MOTHERS AND THEIR SCREAMING KIDS. THOSE PLACES ARE MADE FOR CHEAPSKATES LIKE ME!
007
P-Q

AT LEAST THERE I COULDA BOUGHT THIS CARPET CLEANER FOR FORTY-PERCENT-LESS!!!
XKE
@#9

AND WHERE THE HELL DID I PARK MY CAR?!?!?
XKE
@#9

THIS MUST BE WHAT HELL IS LIKE.....WHERE FAILED SUBURBANITES LIKE MYSELF HAVE TO WANDER AROUND PARKING GARAGES IN SEARCH OF THEIR CARS FOR ALL ETERNITY...

LATER...
BEEP!
HONK!
HONK!
@#!?!#!
BEEP BEEP!
...NOW I WISH I NEVER FOUND MY CAR! LOOK AT ALL THIS TRAFFIC!!! WHERE DID ALL THESE PEOPLE COME FROM?
@#?!@!!
HONK!
BEEP! BEEP!
HONK! HONK!
BEEP,

HONK!
BEEP! BEEP! BEEP!
BEEEP!
@!!#@!
IT LOOKS LIKE THEY'RE ALL HEADING FOR THE MALL! I SURE WISH THERE WAS SOME WAY I COULD TELL THEM ALL TO FORGET IT, GO HOME, IT'S A BIG RIP-OFF!!!
BEEP! BEEP! HONK! BEEP!
%#@!?! BEEP!!
HONK!
HONK!

HONK
HONK!
HONK!
HONK!
HONK!
HONK!
HONK!
C'MON MISTER! MOVE IT!!!
I DON'T GET IT. I KEEP HONKING AT THIS GUY BUT HE STILL KEEPS PUTZING ALONG!!!
HONK
HONK!
HONK!
HONK
HONK!
HONK!
HONK!

UH-OH! HE'S GOT A "HONK IF YOU LOVE JESUS" BUMPER STICKER!
HE PROBABLY THINKS I'M ANOTHER JESUS FREAK!

I HATE JESUS CHRIST'S GUTS, YOU BORN-AGAIN BONEHEAD!!

?
!
OH MY!
NOW GET YER HOLY-ROLLIN' ASS OUT OF MY WAY!!!

OH-NO, THEY'RE GANGING UP ON ME!
...I HAVE A FRIEND IN JEE-ZUZ...
YA CAN'T WIN!
CLICK!

LATER, AT HOME...
SO HOW WAS YOUR "HOLIDAY AT THE MALL"?
TERRIBLE. I'M ALL CRANKY NOW.
TOLD YOU SO, DIDN'T I?
YES, YOU TOLD ME SO!... HERE, I GOT YOU SOME CARPET CLEANER...
GEE, THANKS.

SO HOW WAS WORK TODAY?
DON'T ASK.
UH-OH. THE CUSTOMERS GOT ON YOUR NERVES AGAIN?
YOU'D BETTER BELIEVE THEY GOT ON MY NERVES...

OUR CUSTOMERS THINK THEY'RE SUCH KNOW-IT-ALLS, BUT THEY'RE NOTHIN' BUT A BUNCH OF IGNORANT, MIDDLE-CLASS REDNECKS!
NOTHING'S WORSE THAN AN ILLITERATE, UN-CULTURED SLOB WITH A LITTLE BIT OF MONEY TO SPEND!
IT'S A DEADLY COMBINATION ALRIGHT. THEY JUST WASTE IT ON EXPENSIVE TOYS LIKE R.V.S AND SATELLITE DISHES.

THAT REMINDS ME; DID YOU RENT ANY MOVIES FOR OUR V.C.R?
UH, NO, I DIDN'T. LOOKS LIKE ANOTHER EVENING OF WATCHING LOUSY STUPID T.V. SHOWS AGAIN.

THAT EVENING...
WELL, THE "COSBY SHOW" WAS AS PREACHY AND PHONEY AS EVER. WHAT'S ON NOW?
"FAMILY TIES." DON'T YOU HAVE THE THURSDAY NIGHT LINE-UP MEMORIZED BY NOW?
AAAH... THEY CHANGE THEIR SCHEDULES SO MUCH THESE DAYS I DON'T TRY TO REMEMBER WHAT'S ON

MICHAEL J. FOX IS PRETTY FUNNY ON THIS SHOW, BUT HE ALWAYS TURNS INTO A WIMPY SAP AT THE END.
THAT'S WHAT HAPPENS TO THE PEOPLE WE LIKE ON EVERY SHOW!
...SURE, I'LL ACT "SENSITIVE," BUT IT'LL COST YA !... HA HA HA HA...

YEAH, THAT'S RIGHT! THE "OBNOXIOUS" CHARACTERS AT LEAST HAVE THE NERVE TO SAY WHAT THEY THINK, BUT THE "NICE" CHARACTERS ALWAYS GRIND 'EM DOWN AND MAKE 'EM GIVE-IN IN THE END!
LIKE RIGHT NOW ALEX'S MOTHER IS GIVING HIM THE WEEKLY "SPEECH". I HATE MEREDITH BAXTER-BIRNEY. REMEMBER "BRIDGET LOVES BERNIE"? WHAT A NIGHTMARE THAT SHOW WAS!
...ALEX, YOU MUST LEARN TO RESPECT OTHER PEOPLE'S FEELINGS...

Y'KNOW, WE DON'T HAVE TO WATCH T.V. EVERYNIGHT...
YES WE DO. WE HAVE TO WATCH IN ORDER TO REMIND OURSELVES OF WHAT GARBAGE THE REST OF THE WORLD LIKES, AND HOW MUCH SMARTER WE ARE THAN EVERYBODY ELSE.

YEAH, I GUESS IT IS KINDA FUN TO PUT IT DOWN...
...OH JOY, "HILL STREET BLUES" IS ON. LET'S SEE HOW MANY "FAULTY DIGESTIVE TRACT" JOKES THEY MAKE IN THIS EPISODE. RIGHT HON'?

...I SAID RIGHT HON'?
...HEY, ARE YOU ASLEEP?.
...HUH?
..ARE YA?
ZZZZz...

BOP!

OH, I'M SORRY! I WAS HAVING A BAD DREAM ABOUT WORK!
YEAH, I GUESS YOU WERE.
UH, MAYBE WE SHOULD HIT THE HAY, HUH?

THAT NIGHT...

ARE YOU STILL AWAKE?
UH-HUH.

DO YOU THINK EVERYONE HAS AS HARD A TIME DEALING WITH THE STUPIDITY OF LIFE AS WE DO?
I DOUBT IT, BUT YOU NEVER KNOW. SOME PEOPLE MAY HAVE IT WORSE.

I CAN'T IMAGINE IT BEING ANY WORSE THAN THIS.
YOU'RE FEELING THAT BAD ABOUT IT, HUH?

YUP.
WELL, LOOK AT IT THIS WAY: SOMEDAY WE'LL BOTH BE DEAD AND WE WON'T HAVE TO DEAL WITH THE WORLD ANYMORE, AND THE WORLD WON'T HAVE TO DEAL WITH US.

THAT'S A BEAUTIFUL THOUGHT, DEAREST, BUT THERE'S STILL TOMORROW TO CONTEND WITH.
RIGHT, AND THE DAY AFTER THAT. OH WELL, I GUESS WE'LL JUST HAVE TO FACE IT AS BRAVELY AS WE CAN.

SIGH. I GUESS SO...
ALRIGHT.
...NOW TURN OUT THE LIGHT AND GO TO SLEEP.

CLICK!

A CYNIC'S WORK IS NEVER DONE.
END.

BEEP! BEEP!

CHET AND BUNNY LEEWAY GO FOR A RIDE!
© 1987 P. BAGGE

HEY, BABY! WANNA TAKE A SPIN?!
WOW! YOUR COUSIN'S CORVETTE! HOW'D YOU GET HIM TO LET YOU BORROW IT?!

EASY! I TOLD HIM IT WAS OUR ANNIVERSARY, SO HE LENT IT TO US FOR THE DAY AS A PRESENT!
BUT OUR ANNIVERSARY, WAS LAST WEEK!

WAS IT? I GUESS I FORGOT.
THAT'S OKAY, SO DID I. BUT WHO CARES?...
WE'RE GOING FOR A RIDE IN A 1960 CORVETTE CONVERTIBLE!
YIP-PAY!

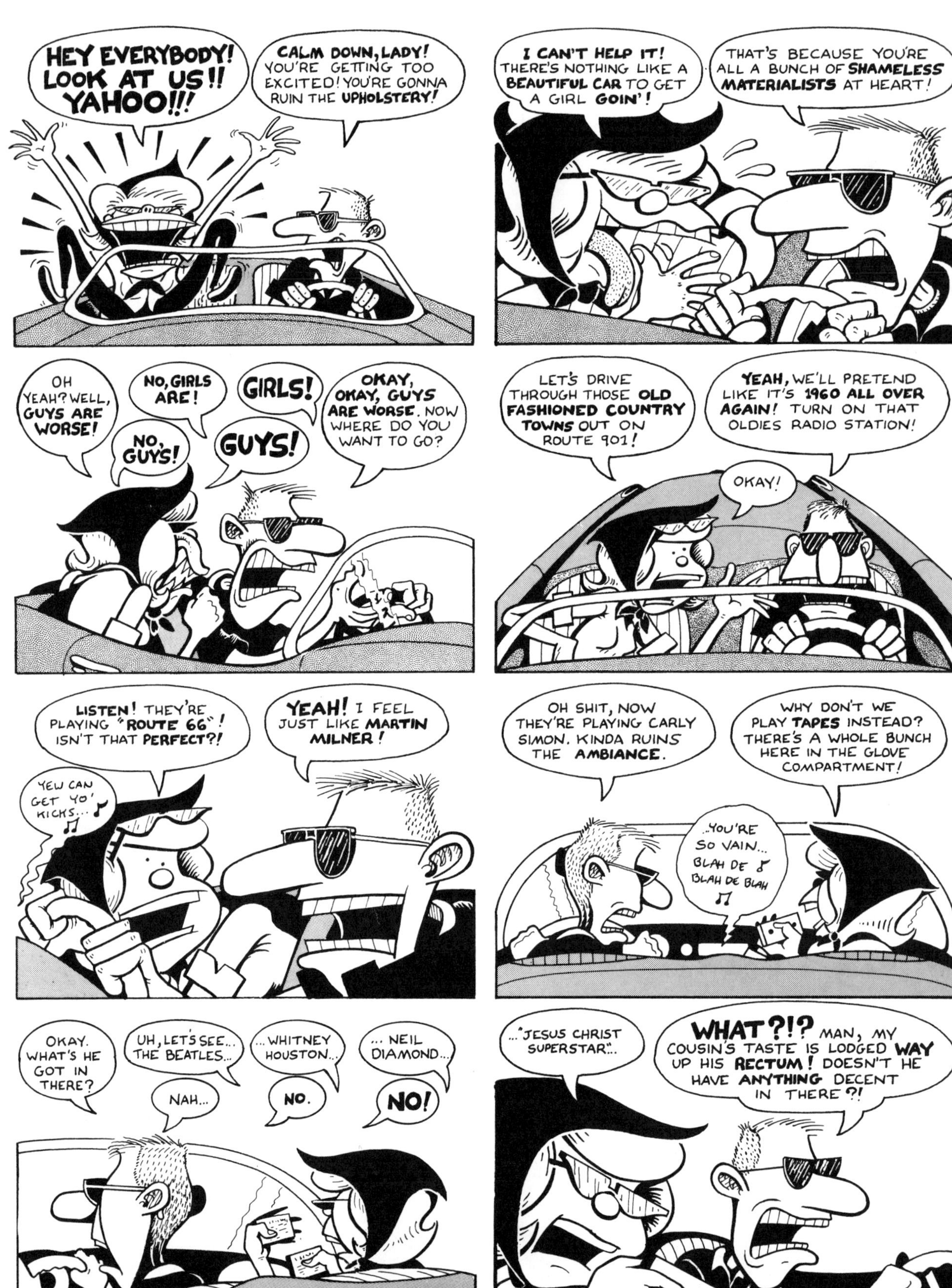

HEY EVERYBODY! LOOK AT US!! YAHOO!!!
CALM DOWN, LADY! YOU'RE GETTING TOO EXCITED! YOU'RE GONNA RUIN THE UPHOLSTERY!
I CAN'T HELP IT! THERE'S NOTHING LIKE A BEAUTIFUL CAR TO GET A GIRL GOIN'!
THAT'S BECAUSE YOU'RE ALL A BUNCH OF SHAMELESS MATERIALISTS AT HEART!
OH YEAH? WELL, GUYS ARE WORSE!
NO, GIRLS ARE!
GIRLS!
OKAY, OKAY, GUYS ARE WORSE. NOW WHERE DO YOU WANT TO GO?
NO, GUYS!
GUYS!
LET'S DRIVE THROUGH THOSE OLD FASHIONED COUNTRY TOWNS OUT ON ROUTE 901!
YEAH, WE'LL PRETEND LIKE IT'S 1960 ALL OVER AGAIN! TURN ON THAT OLDIES RADIO STATION!
OKAY!
LISTEN! THEY'RE PLAYING "ROUTE 66"! ISN'T THAT PERFECT?!
YEAH! I FEEL JUST LIKE MARTIN MILNER!
YEW CAN GET YO' KICKS...
OH SHIT, NOW THEY'RE PLAYING CARLY SIMON. KINDA RUINS THE AMBIANCE.
WHY DON'T WE PLAY TAPES INSTEAD? THERE'S A WHOLE BUNCH HERE IN THE GLOVE COMPARTMENT!
...YOU'RE SO VAIN... BLAH DE BLAH DE BLAH
OKAY. WHAT'S HE GOT IN THERE?
UH, LET'S SEE... THE BEATLES...
...WHITNEY HOUSTON...
... NEIL DIAMOND...
NAH...
NO.
NO!
..."JESUS CHRIST SUPERSTAR"...
WHAT?!? MAN, MY COUSIN'S TASTE IS LODGED WAY UP HIS RECTUM! DOESN'T HE HAVE ANYTHING DECENT IN THERE?!

WELL, HERE'S ONE BY STEPPENWOLF...
SIGH I GUESS IT'LL HAVE TO DO...

LATER...

OH WOW! WE'RE CRUISIN' THE "STRIP"! ISN'T THIS CLASSIC?!
I DONNO...I'M STARTING TO FEEL A BIT VULNERABLE RIDING IN A CONVERTIBLE... I CAN'T WAIT TO GET OUT OF TOWN...
BEEP! BEEP!
HONK!
IT'S ALRIGHT, HEY LAWDY MAMA...
VROOOM!

JEEZ, TAKE A LOOK AT THAT BOMB NEXT TO US. THERE MUST BE A DOZEN TEENAGERS PACKED INTO THAT THING.
YEAH, AND LISTEN TO THAT MUFFLER! WHY DO TEENAGERS ALWAYS HAVE BUSTED MUFFLERS?
RUMBLE... RUMBLE RUMBLE RUMB... BRUMB BRUMB VRUMB...

VROOM! VROOM!
RUMBLE... RUMBLE... BRUMBLE...
THEY'RE ALL DRINKING TOO... CRAZY KIDS... THEY'RE GONNA GET THEMSELVES KILLED...

DO I LOOK LIKE A BUG?
WHAT? A BUG?!? NO, WHY?
VROOOOM!

ONE OF THOSE KIDS SAID I LOOKED LIKE A BUG. THEY WERE LAUGHING AND POINTING AT ME...
HOW DO YOU KNOW WHAT THEY WERE SAYING? YOU COULDN'T HEAR THEM!

I COULD READ THEIR LIPS... OH MY GOD! I DO LOOK LIKE A BUG!!! I'M TAKING THESE STUPID GLASSES OFF!
HAW! HAW! HAW! HAW!

GRRRRR... I HATE TEENAGERS!
SO DO I. THE MAKE ME FEEL OLD.

THEY DO? WHY?
BECAUSE IT'S ONLY BEEN TEN YEARS SINCE I'VE BEEN A TEENAGER, BUT IT FEELS MORE LIKE A MILLION YEARS! I CAN'T BELIEVE I'M THE SAME PERSON, I'VE CHANGED SO MUCH SINCE THEN.

WELL I HATE 'EM BECAUSE THEY'RE SO STUPID! ESPECIALLY TEENS THESE DAYS!
OH, C'MON NOW! THEY'RE STILL JUST KIDS, FOR GOODNESS SAKES! WE WERE PRETTY NAIVE OURSELVES WHEN WE WERE NINETEEN!

OH, I DON'T KNOW ABOUT THAT. I THINK WE WERE PRETTY SLICK, COMPARED TO MOST OF THE KIDS OUR AGE. I MEAN, MOST OF OUR HOMETOWN FRIENDS WERE HAVING BABIES ALREADY, TRAPPED INTO DEAD-END JOBS, IN DEBT UP TO THEIR ELBOWS. IT WAS GRIM...
RIGHT, AND A LOT OF OUR "BOHEMIAN" FRIENDS BECAME JUNKIES, OR COMMITTED SUICIDE, OR DIED OF AIDS. IT KINDA MAKES ME FEEL LIKE WE'RE "SURVIVORS" OR SOMETHING.
YEAH, THOSE WERE CRAZY DAYS. BUT THEY WERE FUN, TOO. LOTS OF GOOD MUSIC WAS COMING OUT BACK THEN...

YEAH, WELL, SOME OF IT WAS ALL RIGHT...
"ALL RIGHT"?!? SOME OF THE BEST ROCK AND ROLL EVER MADE...
THE BEST, HUH? THEN WHY DID YOU GIVE AWAY ALL YOUR "CLASH" AND "TALKING HEADS" RECORDS ONLY A FEW YEARS AFTER YOU BOUGHT THEM?!
OH, UH... WELL, I GOT SICK OF THOSE GUYS... BESIDES, THEY SOLD OUT!

"SOLD OUT"? HA! YOU MEAN THEY GOT POPULAR!
SAME DIFFERENCE! NOTHING GETS TO BE BIG-TIME IN THIS COUNTRY UNLESS AND UNTIL IT'S WATERED-DOWN AND MADE PALPABLE FOR THE MASSES!

IT'S THE SAME WITH FOOD! MOST PEOPLE CAN'T HANDLE SPICY, AUTHENTIC MEXICAN FOOD, BUT THEY ALL FLOCK LIKE SHEEP TO THESE TACO BELLS FOR A CARDBOARD VERSION OF IT!
WELL, YOU CAN'T HANDLE REAL MEXICAN FOOD EITHER, BUBBY!
TACO BELL

OKAY, SO I'M A HYPOCRITE! SO I'M JUST ANOTHER UGLY AMERICAN, TOO! SO FUCK ME!!!
YEAH, FUCK YOU...

OOH! OOH! STOP THE CAR! QUICK!
WHY?! WHAT'S THE MATTER?

LOOK! A GARAGE SALE!
OH NO! WE AIN'T GOIN' TO NO CRUMMY GARAGE SALES!
SALE
SALE

AW, C'MON! THEY LOOK LIKE THEY GOT GOOD STUFF!
WHERE?! ALL I SEE ARE THE USUAL BUSTED LAMPS AND BEAT-UP BOARD GAMES! FORGET IT!

I DON'T KNOW WHAT IT IS ABOUT YOU AND GARAGE SALES...
...THERE'S ANOTHER ONE... *SIGH*

OKAY, I'LL MAKE YOU A DEAL. IF WE SEE ANY SECOND-HAND STORES OR FLEA MARKETS OUT IN THE COUNTRY WE'LL STOP AND LOOK, BUT LET'S AVOID THESE JUNKY SUBURBAN SALES!
OKAY...

LATER, OUT IN THE BOONDOCKS...
THERE'S A NICE LITTLE STORE. LET'S CHECK IT OUT!
SECOND HAND ROSE

DARN, IT'S CLOSED.
IT SEEMS LIKE THESE PLACES ARE ALWAYS CLOSED. I DON'T KNOW HOW THEY STAY IN BUSINESS.

OH WELL, SINCE WE'RE HERE LET'S DRIVE AROUND THE TOWN; EXPLORE THESE OLD BACK ROADS...
IT IS REAL NICE ON THESE OLD COUNTRY ROADS... SOMETIMES I THINK I'D LIKE TO LIVE OUT HERE...

YEAH, IT'S SO CALM AND QUIET OUT HERE...
OH MY GOD! LOOK OUT!!

WHAT?!? WHAT IS IT?!
SOMEONE'S POINTING A SHOTGUN AT US FROM THAT WINDOW!

HOLY SHIT! I DON'T BELIEVE IT!
CHET! LOOK OUT FOR THAT TRUCK!
BEEP!
BEEP!

BAHROOM!
YEOW!!
SWERVE!

WATCH WHERE YOU'RE GOING, YOU GODDAMN REDNECK!
LET'S GET OUT OF THIS SHITHOLE TOWN!

STUPID INBRED YAHOOS! I HOPE THEY ALL ROT IN HELL!
I'D RATHER DIE THAN LIVE AMONGST THESE BACKWARD DIRT FARMERS!

WELP, WHERE TO NOW?
THERE'S A SIGN FOR SNOQUALMIE FALLS. THAT'S SUPPOSED TO BE A PRETTY PLACE.
SNOQUALMIE FALLS IT IS, THEN.
SNOQUALMIE FALLS 6 MILES
NORTH BEND 12 MILES

HERE WE ARE.
WELCOME T
SNOQUALM
FALLS

PRETTY.

HEY, WHY SO GLUM, CHUM?

NOTHING. I'M FINE.
NO YOU'RE NOT. YOU'RE DEPRESSED. I CAN TELL.

YEAH, RIGHT, HOW DARE I BE DEPRESSED ON SUCH A SUNSHINY DAY, AT THIS OFFICIALLY SANCTIONED "BEAUTIFUL SPOT"! A SPOT SO BEAUTIFUL THAT PEOPLE FEEL MOVED TO LEAVE THEIR GARBAGE ALL OVER THE PLACE JUST TO PROVE THEY WERE HERE!

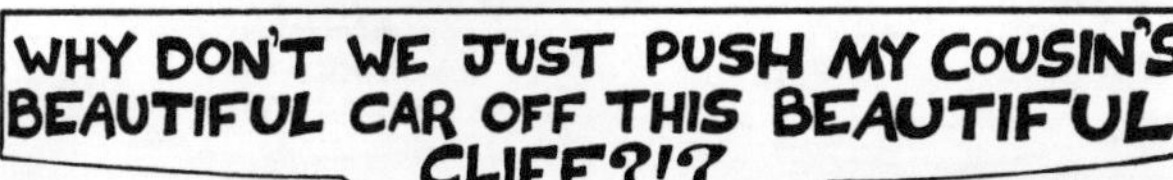

OKAY, SO I'M DEPRESSED. SO WHAT.
Y'KNOW, SOMETIMES I CAN'T FIGURE YOU OUT. HERE WE ARE ON OUR DAY OFF, IT'S A BEAUTIFUL DAY, WE'VE GOT A BEAUTIFUL CAR, WE'RE SITTING IN A BEAUTIFUL SPOT, AND YOU'RE DEPRESSED.

WHY DON'T WE JUST PUSH MY COUSIN'S BEAUTIFUL CAR OFF THIS BEAUTIFUL CLIFF?!?

I DON'T KNOW, WHY DON'T WE?

WE SHOULD, SHOULDN'T WE? MY ASSHOLE COUSIN DOESN'T DESERVE TO OWN A CAR LIKE THAT ANYWAY!
I SUPPOSE YOU DESERVE IT?
ME? NAH...I FEEL KINDA FOOLISH DRIVING IN IT...
I DONNO... I NEVER HAVE FUN DOING THINGS THAT ARE SUPPOSED TO BE "FUN"!
IT'S LIKE THE MORE EXPENSIVE OR EXOTIC SOMETHING IS, THE MORE FUN IT'S SUPPOSED TO BE.
I KNOW WHAT YOU MEAN. YOU FEEL LIKE YOU'RE COMMITTING A CRIME IF YOU DON'T ENJOY DOING SOMETHING YOU'RE SUPPOSED TO ENJOY!
EXACTLY!
YOU KNOW WHAT KIND OF STUFF I LIKE TO DO THE MOST? I LIKE WHEN WE'RE HARDLY DOING NOTHING, LIKE ON SATURDAY MORNINGS WHEN WE'RE JUST HANGING AROUND IN OUR PAJAMAS EATING ONE EGGO AFTER ANOTHER, AND THE T.V. IS BLARING AWAY BUT WE'RE NOT EVEN WATCHING IT!
HMMM...
...OR LIKE WHEN WE'RE LYING IN BED READING TRASHY MAGAZINES AND LISTENING TO THE MARINERS LOSE ON THE RADIO...
...OR NATIONAL GEO-GRAPHICS. I LIKE TO READ OLD NATIONAL GEOGRAPHICS WHILE LISTENING TO THE MARINERS LOSE ON THE RADIO.
I GUESS WE'RE PRETTY WEIRD, HUH?
YEAH, WELL, I DON'T KNOW... I WOULDN'T BE SURPRISED IF EVERY-ONE BASICALLY FELT THE SAME WAY THAT WE DO, BUT WE'VE ALL BEEN BRAINWASHED BY ADVERTISING AND OTHER POWERS THAT BE...
WELL, I LIKE TO THINK WE'RE THE ONLY PEOPLE WHO THINK LIKE WE DO! WE'RE NON-CONFORMISTS, MAN!
RIGHT ON, MAN!
OOOH! WHAT A BEE-YOO-TEE-FUL SUNSET!
HA! HA! HA! WHERE'S MY POLAROID?!
END.

CHET + BUNNY LEEWAY in
BEDRIDDEN
SPORTS
© 1988 BY PETER BAGGE

YAWWWNN!

WHAT TIME IS IT?
SPORTS

2:30.

TWO-THIRTY?! HOLY CRUD!! I CAN'T BELIEVE WE'VE BEEN LYING IN BED ALL DAY, DOING NOTHING!

WE HAVEN'T BEEN DOING NOTHING. WE'VE BEEN READING THE PAPER.
OH, YOU KNOW WHAT I MEAN! I MEAN SOMETHING ...PRODUCTIVE!

SO WHAT. RELAX. YOU WORK HARD. YOU DESERVE A DAY OFF FROM EVERY-THING.
BUT WE STAYED IN BED ALL DAY YESTERDAY TOO! AND ALL OF LAST WEEKEND!

MY GOD. YOU'RE RIGHT.
WE DON'T DO ANY-THING ANYMORE! THIS IS GETTING PATHETIC!

WELL, WHAT WOULD YOU RATHER BE DOING? WE NEVER FEEL LIKE DOING ANY OF THE THINGS WE USED TO DO...
OH, I DON'T KNOW. ALL I KNOW IS THAT WHEN I GO BACK TO WORK IT SEEMS LIKE I DIDN'T EVEN HAVE A WEEKEND!

I KNOW I WORK HARD AND DESERVE TO TAKE IT EASY ON MY DAYS OFF AND ALL THAT KIND OF STUFF, BUT THIS IS RIDICULOUS! IT'S LIKE I DON'T EVEN KNOW WHAT I'M WORKING FOR ANYMORE! OUR LIVES HAVE BECOME A BIG EMPTY VOID!

WELLLL... MAYBE THIS IS NATURE'S WAY OF TELLING US IT'S TIME TO HAVE A KID...
FUCK THAT SHIT. YOU HAVE A KID!

IT WAS JUST A THOUGHT... HEY! WHERE YA GOING?
I'M GETTING OUT OF BED. I GOTTA DO SOMETHING!

LIKE WHAT? WHAT'S THERE TO DO?
LIKE THE DISHES, FOR ONE THING.

BUT I WAS GONNA DO THE DISHES!
OH YEAH? WHEN?
TOMORROW.
TOMORROW, HAH! SURE!

AW, DON'T GET UP! YOU'RE MAKING ME FEEL LIKE THE LAZY WORTHLESS BUM THAT I AM! WHY DON'T YOU COME BACK HERE SO'S WE CAN BE LAZY WORTHLESS BUMS TOGETHER!
WHY DON'T YOU GET UP AND DO SOME WORK AROUND THE HOUSE? THERE'S A LOT THAT NEEDS TO BE DONE...

WORK....UGGH... I CAN'T.....I DON'T HAVE THE ENERGY ...I CAN'T MOVE...
WELL, WHY DON'T YOU CALL UP SOME OF YOUR FRIENDS AND INVITE THEM OVER? IT SEEMS LIKE YOU HAVEN'T SEEN ANY OF THEM LATELY...

...FRIENDS... WHAT FRIENDS... I DON'T HAVE ANY FRIENDS...
I'M SERIOUS! WHAT ABOUT YOUR LITTLE "BEACH BOYS FAN CLUB"? YOU HAVEN'T GOTTEN TOGETHER WITH THOSE GUYS IN AGES!

WHO, THE WANG BROTHERS?! I'VE SEEN ENOUGH OF THOSE GUYS TO LAST ME A LIFETIME!!
BESIDES, IT USED TO DRIVE YOU BATTY HAVING TO LISTEN TO BEACH BOYS RECORDS ALL DAY!

I KNOW, BUT AT LEAST THEY'RE PEOPLE THAT YOU HAVE SOMETHING IN COMMON WITH! IT MIGHT BE FUN FOR YOU TO SIT AROUND AND SHOOT THE BREEZE WITH THEM AGAIN, AND IT MIGHT HELP SNAP YOU OUT OF THIS FUNK YOU'RE IN!
AAAAH... I DON'T THINK SO...

THERE'S ONLY A FINITE AMOUNT OF THINGS THAT CAN BE SAID ABOUT THE BEACH BOYS. AND ONCE WE INEVITABLY BURN OUT ON THAT SUBJECT, THAT'S WHEN YOU FIND OUT WHAT SOCIAL RETARDS THE WANG BROTHERS ARE!

LIKE, SHERMAN IS CONSTANTLY TALKING ABOUT HIS DEAD WIFE. IT'S SO MORBID! I MEAN, I FEEL SORRY FOR THE GUY, BUT JEEZ, IT'S BEEN SIX YEARS NOW! I WISH HE'D START THINKING ABOUT LIFE FOR A CHANGE!

...AND I ONCE MADE THE MISTAKE OF ASKING ROY WHAT EXACTLY HIS JOB WAS AT MICROSOFT, AND H.. WENT ON FOR AN HOUR BABBLING ABOUT SOME MIDDLE MANAGEMENT COMPUTER ANALYSIS QUALITY CONTROL MUMBO JUMBO. IT WAS ALL I COULD DO TO KEEP MY EYES OPEN!....
SOUNDS LIKE YOUR JOB.

SAY WHAT? MY JOB? WELL...I GUESS SO, BUT AT LEAST I DON'T BORE PEOPLE WITH THE DETAILS...
THAT'S TRUE (EXCEPT FOR ME ANYWAYS)...

..BUT I MUST BE TURNING PEOPLE OFF SOMEHOW, BECAUSE NO-ONE EVER CALLS ME ANY-MORE, EITHER...
NOW THAT'S NOT TRUE! IF YOUR FRIENDS AREN'T CALLING YOU IT'S BECAUSE YOU NEVER CALL THEM!

HEY, I'VE TRIED TO KEEP IN TOUCH WITH MY FRIENDS, BUT LATELY IT JUST DOESN'T SEEM TO BE WORTH THE EFFORT. I GET THIS WEIRD, PARANOID FEELING WHENEVER I TALK TO ANY OF THEM LATELY!
HOW DO YOU MEAN?

WELL, IT'S LIKE I'LL BE IN THE MIDDLE OF SAYING SOMETHING AND NOT BEING TOO AWARE OF WHAT I'M SAYING, WHEN ALL OF A SUDDEN I'LL START TO FEEL THE OTHER PERSON FREEZING UP ON ME, ALMOST IN HORROR, AS IF I'M THE MOST REPULSIVE, INCURABLE CYNIC THEY'VE EVER ENCOUNTERED!
WELL, YOU ARE A CYNIC, BUT I DON'T THINK...

LOOK, I KNOW YOU'RE GONNA TELL ME I'M IMAGINING THINGS, BUT IT'S TRUE!!
THERE SEEMS TO BE THIS GAP GROWING BETWEEN ME AND EVERYONE I KNOW, AND I CAN'T FIGURE OUT WHAT THE PROBLEM IS!
...SOME-TIMES I WONDER IF IT COULD SIMPLY BE THAT THEY'RE GROWING UP AND I'M NOT.
I DON'T THINK THAT MATURITY HAS ANYTHING TO DO WITH IT, BUT IT DOES SEEM LIKE YOU GOTTA WATCH WHAT YOU SAY THESE DAYS. I GET SOME WEIRD "VIBES" TOO WHEN-EVER I DARE TO UTTER AN OPINION...

SO I GUESS THE IDEA IS TO KEEP OUR THOUGHTS TO OURSELVES, HUH?
I GUESS. ONLY I FEEL LIKE I'M DOING THAT MOST OF THE TIME AS IT IS!

MAYBE THE TRICK IS TO GET STUPID. IF WE COULD LOWER OUR INTELLIGENCE SOMEHOW MAYBE WE'D GET ALONG WITH PEOPLE BETTER!
I'D CERTAINLY GET ALONG WITH MY CUSTOMERS BETTER IF I WAS AS DUMB AS THEY ARE!

HA-HA!

I KNOW! WE SHOULD BOTH GET LOBOTOMIES! THEN WE'D BE THE MOST POPULAR COUPLE IN TOWN!
...OR OF COURSE WE COULD DO AS YOU SUGGESTED AND HAVE A KID!..
THEN WHENEVER WE GO TO A PARTY I COULD SIT IN THE KITCHEN WITH ALL THE WOMEN AND TALK ABOUT BABIES ALL EVENING!
THAT'S RIGHT...

... AND THEN YOU CAN SIT IN THE LIVING ROOM OR GO DOWN TO THE "REC ROOM" WITH ALL THE MEN AND WATCH THE "BIG GAME" AND TALK ABOUT NO-THING BUT SPORTS!
RIGHT, SPORTS, SPORTS, SPORTS, THE REAL DRUG OF THE MASSES! I HATE SPORTS!

WHADAYA MEAN, YOU HATE SPORTS? YOU'RE SUCH A BIG BASEBALL FAN!
I FOLLOW IT OUT OF HABIT, BUT I HATE IT AT THE SAME TIME. I HATE EVERTHING THESE DAYS. I'M OVER-WHELMED WITH HATE!
PLOP!

I'M SO CONSUMED WITH HATRED THAT I CAN HARDLY MOVE ...MAYBE THAT'S WHY I CAN'T GET OUT OF BED — HATRED HAS TAKEN OVER MY BODY LIKE A CRIPPLING VIRUS...IT'S COURSING THROUGH MY VEINS...OOZING FROM EVERY ONE OF MY PORES LIKE A THICK, YELLOW BILE.........

OH LORD, HOW DID I EVER GET THIS WAY?! WHY AM I SO FULL OF CONTEMPT? I CAN'T ENJOY OR APPRECIATE ANYTHING ANYMORE! I'M TURNING INTO A MONSTER!
DO YOU WANT TO WATCH SOME T.V.?

T.V.?! ARE YOU KIDDING? I HATE T.V.!! HOW CAN YOU SUGGEST WATCHING T.V. AT A TIME LIKE THIS!...
HEY, I WAS ONLY TRYING TO CHEER YOU UP! DON'T SNAP AT ME!

...SORRY...
WELL, HERE, READ THE MAGAZINE SECTION OF THE NEWSPAPER. YOU ALWAYS GET A BIG LAUGH OUT OF THAT!

YES...THIS PROFILE ON MARLO THOMAS OUGHT TO LIFT MY SPIRITS...
GOOD. I HOPE IT DOES. I'M GONNA GO MAKE SOME PHONE CALLS...

SHEESH, THIS MAGAZINE FEATURES THE SAME CRAPOLA WEEK AFTER WEEK...
LIKE THESE BIOS ON WASHED-UP CELEBRITIES WHO'VE SURVIVED SOME PERSONAL TRAGEDY AND ARE NOW STAGING FABULOUS COME-BACKS...
PARADE
I'VE BEEN TO HELL + BACK AND NOW I'M A STRONGER PERSON FOR IT! BY BIMBO STARLETTA

AND THEN THERE'S THESE STORIES ABOUT SICK AND DISABLED PEOPLE WHO OVERCOME HUGE OBSTACLES THANKS TO THEIR SUPPORTIVE FAMILIES AND THEIR UNSHAKABLE FAITH IN GOD...
5 LIVER TRASPLA DOESN'T STOP LI CINDY GOODWIN FR GOING TO CHUR EVERY DAY! B

...THEN THERE'S THESE FACTS + FIGURES ON THE HIGH RATES OF SUBSTANCE ABUSE IN THIS COUNTRY...
...67% OF ALL GRADE SCHOOLERS ARE CHRONIC ALCOHOLICS... WE'RE ALL GOING TO HELL IN A HAND-BASKET...SO WHAT ELSE IS NEW...
...HEY, WHAT'S THIS?...

OH NO!
WHAT IS IT?! WHAT'S THE MATTER?

LISTEN TO THIS!: "THE LATEST TREND AMONG `BABY-BOOMERS` IS `COCOONING`, WHEREIN YOUNG URBAN COUPLES HAVE BEEN CHOOSING TO STAY HOME BY THEM-SELVES INSTEAD OF GOING OUT AND SOCIALIZING WITH OTHERS. PEOPLE ARE INTO BEING `COUCH POTATOES` THESE DAYS", SAYS MARKET ANALYST MARY JIFFYPOP"...
"MARY JIFFYPOP"?

THAT EVENING...

CHET and BUNNY LEEWAY
in
"PARTY POOPERS"
© 1989 BY P. BAGGE
WE'D BETTER START GETTING READY FOR THE PARTY, CHET.
WHY? IT DOESN'T START FOR ANOTHER FIVE HOURS!

IT'S A BARBEQUE, CHET! AND IT'S STARTED ALREADY!
OH, THE BARBEQUE! I FORGOT ALL ABOUT IT! I THOUGHT YOU WERE TALKING ABOUT YOUR FRIEND'S ART SHOW TONIGHT!

AND I THOUGHT THAT WE DECIDED THAT WE WEREN'T GOING TO THE ART OPENING TONIGHT!
WE DID? WHEN DID WE DECIDE THIS? WAS I IN ON THIS DECISION?

YES, BUT YOU PROBABLY WEREN'T PAYING ATTENTION, AS USUAL. ARE YOU SAYING YOU WANT TO GO TO IT NOW?
WELL, YEAH. IT'D BE A NICE CHANGE OF PACE FROM OUR OH-SO-MIDDLE-CLASS, HUM-DRUM EXISTENCE...

I AGREE, BUT IT'S TOO LATE TO CHANGE YOUR MIND NOW, BECAUSE WE'RE GOING TO THE KOENIG'S BARBEQUE INSTEAD...
AW, BUT I DON'T WANNA GO TO NO BARBEQUE, ESPECIALLY ONE WITH YOUR FRIENDS FROM WORK! I DON'T FEEL LIKE DEALING WITH THOSE CRETINS...

THAT'S WHAT YOU ALWAYS SAY, AND THEN YOU ALWAYS WIND UP HAVING A GOOD TIME!
DO I? THAT'S PROBABLY BECAUSE I ALWAYS GET PLASTERED AT THOSE BARBEQUES!
WALTER KOENIG ALWAYS MAKES SURE THAT EVERYONE ALWAYS HAS A FULL GLASS OF BOOZE IN THEIR MITTS!

IT'S AMAZING WE HAVEN'T GOTTEN KILLED DRIVING HOME FROM ONE OF THEIR SHIN-DIGS...
I KNOW... WALTER HATES TO BE THE ONLY ONE PUKING UNDER THE AZALEA BUSHES...HE WANTS US ALL TO BE DOWN THERE WITH HIM!

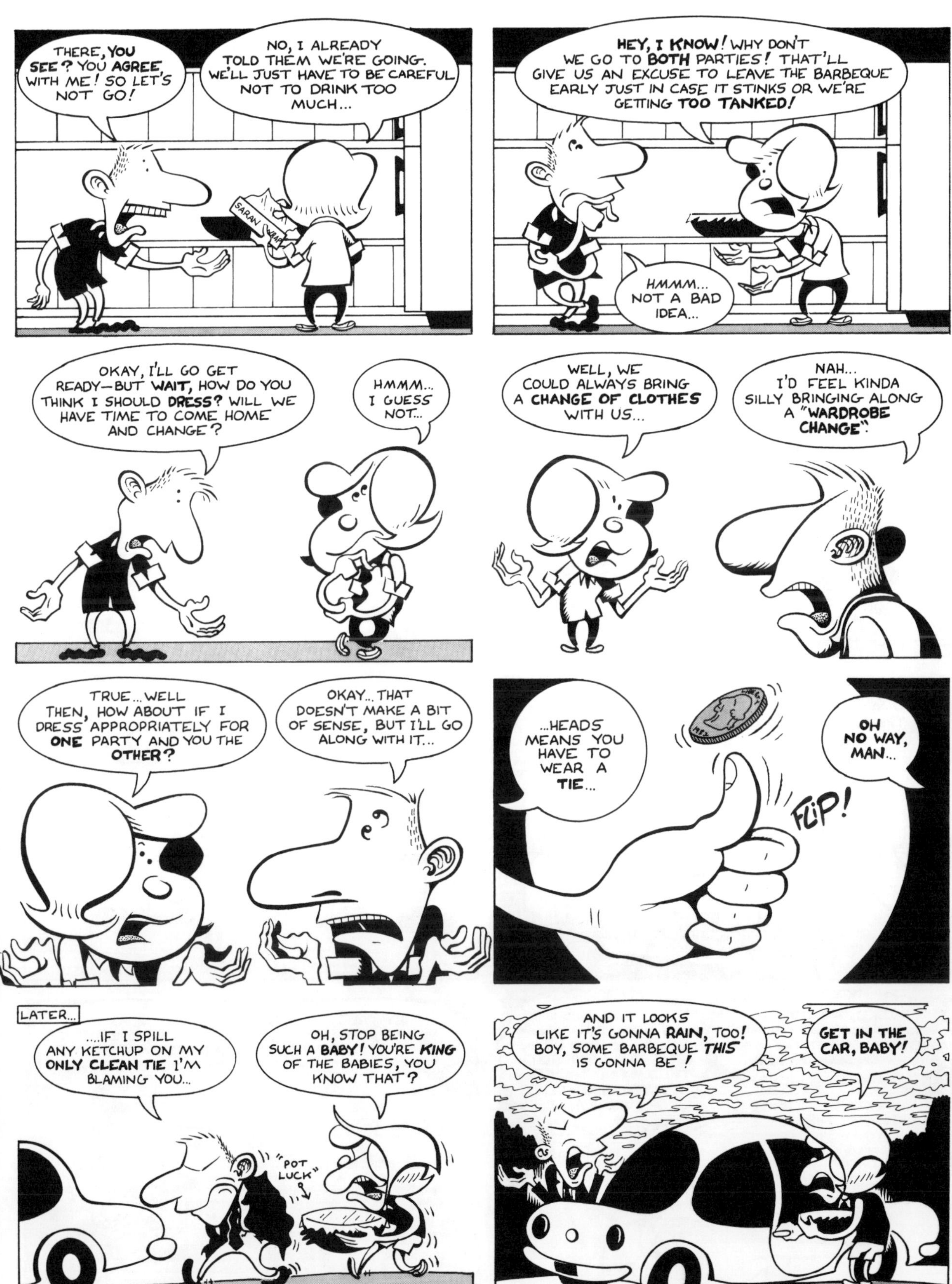

THERE, YOU SEE? YOU AGREE WITH ME! SO LET'S NOT GO!
NO, I ALREADY TOLD THEM WE'RE GOING. WE'LL JUST HAVE TO BE CAREFUL NOT TO DRINK TOO MUCH...
HEY, I KNOW! WHY DON'T WE GO TO BOTH PARTIES! THAT'LL GIVE US AN EXCUSE TO LEAVE THE BARBEQUE EARLY JUST IN CASE IT STINKS OR WE'RE GETTING TOO TANKED!
HMMM... NOT A BAD IDEA...
OKAY, I'LL GO GET READY—BUT WAIT, HOW DO YOU THINK I SHOULD DRESS? WILL WE HAVE TIME TO COME HOME AND CHANGE?
HMMM... I GUESS NOT...
WELL, WE COULD ALWAYS BRING A CHANGE OF CLOTHES WITH US...
NAH... I'D FEEL KINDA SILLY BRINGING ALONG A "WARDROBE CHANGE".
TRUE...WELL THEN, HOW ABOUT IF I DRESS APPROPRIATELY FOR ONE PARTY AND YOU THE OTHER?
OKAY... THAT DOESN'T MAKE A BIT OF SENSE, BUT I'LL GO ALONG WITH IT...
...HEADS MEANS YOU HAVE TO WEAR A TIE...
OH NO WAY, MAN...
FLIP!
LATER...
...IF I SPILL ANY KETCHUP ON MY ONLY CLEAN TIE I'M BLAMING YOU...
OH, STOP BEING SUCH A BABY! YOU'RE KING OF THE BABIES, YOU KNOW THAT?
"POT LUCK"
AND IT LOOKS LIKE IT'S GONNA RAIN, TOO! BOY, SOME BARBEQUE THIS IS GONNA BE!
GET IN THE CAR, BABY!

LATER, AT THE KOENIGS...
GREETINGS, LEEWAYS! I WAS WORRIED YOU WEREN'T GOING TO SHOW UP!
ARE YOU KIDDING? WE WOULDN'T MISS ONE OF YOUR BAR-BEQUES FOR ANYTHING!
RAIN! I KNEW IT!

I GOT THE GRILL GOIN' IN THE GARAGE SINCE IT'S STARTING TO RAIN, BUT WE WON'T LET THAT STOP US FROM HAVING A GOOD TIME, RIGHT?
RIGHT, WALTER...
BUNNY? IS THAT YOU?

HIYA, MITZY.
C'MON UPSTAIRS, BUNNY—GLADYS BROUGHT HER NEW BABY AND SHE'S SO CUTE! YOU'VE GOT TO SEE IT!
OH, HI CHET!
HI...

ALL US GUYS ARE DOWNSTAIRS, CHET... IF WE HURRY WE MIGHT CATCH THE END OF THE BALL GAME...
OH, OKAY... BUT I WANTED TO SEE THE BABY TOO!

♪ ..BORN IN THE U.S.A... ♪
...MEN ON FIRST AND SECOND...
SCOTCH AND SODA, RIGHT?
HUH?

THAT'S YOUR USUAL, RIGHT? SCOTCH AND SODA?
COMING RIGHT UP!
OH...YEAH, RIGHT, BUT...

JEEZ, WE JUST WALKED IN THE DOOR AND ALREADY THEY GOT THE MEN AND WOMEN SEGREGATED...
...I SURE WISH IT WASN'T RAINING— I FEEL COOPED UP IN HERE...THEY GOT BOTH THE T.V. AND THE C.D. PLAYER CRANKED UP FULL BLAST!
HEY CHET, WHAT'S WITH THE TIE? YOU GOIN' PUNK ON US OR SOMETHIN'?

HEY FRED, AND NO, I'M NOT GOING "PUNK."
OH, I MEANT "NEW WAVE", 'CUZ THERE'S A DIFFERENCE, RIGHT?

NO, BUT YOU'RE CLOSE. I'M GOING "DISCO".
IS THIS GUY PULLING MY LEG OR IS HE REALLY THAT OUT OF IT?
SERIOUSLY? I MEAN, ARE YOU GUYS GOING OUT DANCING AFTER THIS?
NO, BUT WE ARE GOING TO THIS, UH, "THING" LATER...THIS, ER, "FUNCTION"..
I CAN'T BELIEVE I'M AFRAID TO TELL THIS GUY I'M GOING TO A GALLERY OPENING!
THEN AGAIN, WHO COULD BLAME ME?
UH-HUH...
HEY FREDDIE, TELL EVERYONE THOSE ALBANIAN JOKES YOU WERE TELLING ME YESTERDAY!
OKAY, LET ME SEE IF I REMEMBER THEM...
OKAY, LISTEN UP EVERYBODY! THIS ALBANIAN IS WALKING ALONG THE BEACH, RIGHT? AND HE FINDS THIS GENIE BOTTLE, SEE? SO HE PICKS IT UP...
OH GREAT, HERE WE GO WITH THE RACIST/SEXIST HUMOR FESTIVAL AGAIN...
MEANWHILE, UPSTAIRS...
.."KNOTS LANDING" IS THE ONLY ONE THAT'S STILL GOOD, BUT I STILL WATCH "DYNASTY," IF ONLY FOR THE OUTFITS...
...BARBARA BUSH IS TOO OLD LOOKING TO BE THE FIRST LADY, IF YOU ASK ME...
...SO WHEN JENNY CAME DOWN WITH A 103° FEVER, I FIGURED I'D BETTER CALL THE DOC, EVEN THOUGH THEY CHARGE AN ARM AND A LEG...
...I TOLD MY HUSBAND A THOUSAND TIMES TO GET THAT CAR CHECKED! AND NOW WE'RE STUCK WITH JUST THE VAN AND THE OLD CHEVETTE!
YAWN...
URP!
MO-OM!
BRUMM..
PAMPERS
IT'S BAD ENOUGH THAT I HAVE TO LISTEN TO THIS CONVERSATION ALL DAY AT WORK, BUT NOW I GOTTA SPEND MY DAY OFF LISTENING TO IT!
WHAT'S THE POINT OF ALL THESE GET-TOGETHER'S IF ALL WE'RE GONNA DO IS BORE EACH OTHER TO DEATH!
...I KNEW THAT KID WAS GONNA WIND UP IN JAIL! I TOLD HIS PARENTS MONTHS AGO THAT HIM AND HIS FRIENDS WERE UP TO NO GOOD...
THAT WOMAN REALLY TAKES THE CAKE. SHE JUST SITS THERE AND PONTIFICATES FROM DAWN 'TIL DUSK...
BLAH! BLAH! BLAH! BLAH!
BLAH! BLAH! BLAH!

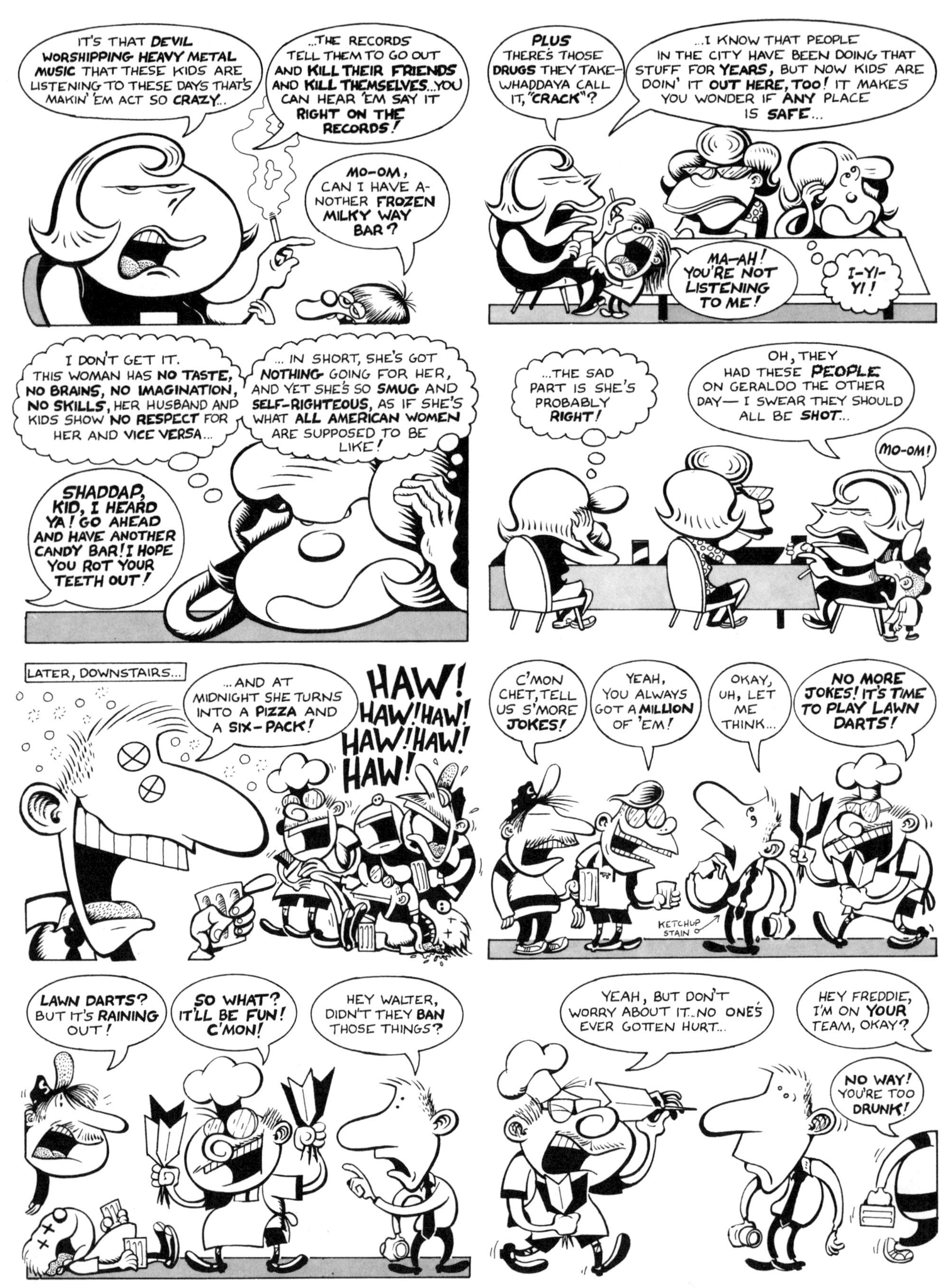

IT'S THAT DEVIL WORSHIPPING HEAVY METAL MUSIC THAT THESE KIDS ARE LISTENING TO THESE DAYS THAT'S MAKIN' 'EM ACT SO CRAZY...
...THE RECORDS TELL THEM TO GO OUT AND KILL THEIR FRIENDS AND KILL THEMSELVES...YOU CAN HEAR 'EM SAY IT RIGHT ON THE RECORDS!
MO-OM, CAN I HAVE A- NOTHER FROZEN MILKY WAY BAR?
PLUS THERE'S THOSE DRUGS THEY TAKE— WHADDAYA CALL IT, "CRACK"?
...I KNOW THAT PEOPLE IN THE CITY HAVE BEEN DOING THAT STUFF FOR YEARS, BUT NOW KIDS ARE DOIN' IT OUT HERE, TOO! IT MAKES YOU WONDER IF ANY PLACE IS SAFE...
MA-AH! YOU'RE NOT LISTENING TO ME!
I-YI- YI!
I DON'T GET IT. THIS WOMAN HAS NO TASTE, NO BRAINS, NO IMAGINATION, NO SKILLS, HER HUSBAND AND KIDS SHOW NO RESPECT FOR HER AND VICE VERSA...
...IN SHORT, SHE'S GOT NOTHING GOING FOR HER, AND YET SHE'S SO SMUG AND SELF-RIGHTEOUS, AS IF SHE'S WHAT ALL AMERICAN WOMEN ARE SUPPOSED TO BE LIKE!
SHADDAP, KID, I HEARD YA! GO AHEAD AND HAVE ANOTHER CANDY BAR! I HOPE YOU ROT YOUR TEETH OUT!
...THE SAD PART IS SHE'S PROBABLY RIGHT!
OH, THEY HAD THESE PEOPLE ON GERALDO THE OTHER DAY— I SWEAR THEY SHOULD ALL BE SHOT...
MO-OM!
LATER, DOWNSTAIRS...
...AND AT MIDNIGHT SHE TURNS INTO A PIZZA AND A SIX-PACK!
HAW! HAW! HAW! HAW! HAW! HAW!
C'MON CHET, TELL US S'MORE JOKES!
YEAH, YOU ALWAYS GOT A MILLION OF 'EM!
OKAY, UH, LET ME THINK...
NO MORE JOKES! IT'S TIME TO PLAY LAWN DARTS!
KETCHUP STAIN
LAWN DARTS? BUT IT'S RAINING OUT!
SO WHAT? IT'LL BE FUN! C'MON!
HEY WALTER, DIDN'T THEY BAN THOSE THINGS?
YEAH, BUT DON'T WORRY ABOUT IT...NO ONE'S EVER GOTTEN HURT...
HEY FREDDIE, I'M ON YOUR TEAM, OKAY?
NO WAY! YOU'RE TOO DRUNK!

BACK UPSTAIRS...
HI VICKY! BOY, AM I GLAD YOU SHOWED UP!
WHY ARE YOU SITTING OVER HERE BY YOURSELF?
BECAUSE THE CONVERSATION HERE WAS DRIVING ME CRAZY! EVERYONE IS BEING BORING AND STUPID!
GOOD, THEN WE CAN SIT HERE AND MAKE FUN OF EVERYBODY ELSE! I'M IN A PISS ASS MOOD MYSELF!
CHOMP!
WHY ARE YOU IN A PISS-ASS MOOD?
AAH, ME AND MY BOYFRIEND HAD ANOTHER FIGHT. HE WAS GETTING ON MY CASE AS USUAL, SO I FINALLY TOLD HIM THE REASON HE'S SO HYPERCRITICAL IS BECAUSE HE'S GOT A PUNY PECKER. THAT SHUT HIM UP IN A HURRY!
VICKY! THAT'S MEAN!
YEAH, I KNOW...THE TRUTH HURTS.
...AND SPEAKING OF PENIS SIZES, DID YOU SEE THAT BIG BLACK GUY THAT CAME INTO WORK YESTERDAY?
SEE HIM? HOW COULD I MISS HIM!? I WAS EYE-LEVEL WITH THAT OBSCENELY HUGE CROTCH OF HIS!
HE MUST BE A PROFESSIONAL ATHLETE OR SOMETHING...
PROFESSIONAL STUD IS MORE LIKE IT... COULD YOU IMAGINE GETTING PORKED BY A DICK THAT BIG?
OF COURSE I WOULD NEVER HAVE SEX WITH A BLACK MAN, BUT STILL...
WHAT? ARE YOU SERIOUS?
OF COURSE I'M SERIOUS! WHY, ARE YOU SAYING THAT YOU WOULD?
WELL, YEAH, SURE... DEPENDING ON THE SITUATION, OF COURSE...
WOW BUNNY, I DIDN'T KNOW YOU HAD A "THING" FOR DARK MEAT! DOES CHET KNOW ABOUT THIS?
NO! I MEAN, WHAT I MEAN IS I...

SO TELL ME BUNNY, IF THAT GUY COMES BACK IN AGAIN ARE YOU GOING TO SEDUCE HIM? OR HAVE YOU DONE "IT" WITH HIM ALREADY?
C'MON BUNNY, YOU CAN TELL ME...
TELL YOU WHAT? WHAT'S THE BIG SECRET?
...BUNNY'S IN LOVE WITH A NEGRO...
WHAT? SHE HAS A BLACK BOYFRIEND? BUT ISN'T SHE MARRIED?
CHET WAS RIGHT— MY WORK FRIENDS ARE A BUNCH OF CRETINS!
??
EMBARRASSED
LATER, IN THE BACK YARD...
WHAT ARE YOU GUYS DOING OUTSIDE IN THE RAIN? AND WHERE'S CHET?
HE'S WITH WALTER OVER BY THE AZALEA BUSHES.
WHAT?!
OH NO! CHET, YOU'RE NOT SICK AGAIN, ARE YOU?!
DON'T WORRY. HE'LL BE ALL RIGHT.
WHAT HAPPENED?
I GOT HIT IN THE HEAD WITH A LAWN DART... IT'S NO BIG DEAL...
AT LEAST NO BLOOD IS GUSHING OUT LIKE IT WAS BEFORE. YOU SHOULD'VE SEEN IT, BUNNY!
FIRST AID
I THINK WE OUGHT TO LEAVE NOW, CHESTER...
AW, WHY? I'M HAVING A LOT OF FUN! CAN'T WE STAY A LITTLE LONGER?
BUT WE AGREED NOT TO STAY TOO LONG, REMEMBER? IT WAS YOUR IDEA, REMEMBER?
YEAH, YOU'RE RIGHT...LET ME SAY GOODBYE TO THE GUYS...
"THE GUYS", GOOD GRIEF!
HEY CHET, WHERE YA GOING? DID THE GAME GET A LITTLE TOO ROUGH FOR YA?
WELL, WE HAVE THIS PRIOR ENGAGEMENT DOWNTOWN, UH...
WE'RE GOING TO AN ART SHOW!
HA-HA!

AN ART SHOW?! WELL WHOOP-DE DO!
BUY ME A PRETTY PICTURE, WON'T YOU CHET?
HAW! HAW!
DID YOU HAVE TO TELL THEM WHERE WE WERE GOING?
OH FER THE LOVE OF PETE!

CHET, ARE YOU FEELING OKAY? YOU CAN HARDLY WALK!
I'M FINE, JUST A LITTLE BLOOD LOSS, THAT'S ALL...

ARE YOU SURE YOU CAN DRIVE? HOW MANY DRINKS DID YOU HAVE?
I HAD TWO... OR TWENTY... SOMEWHERE'S AROUND THERE...
BUT DON'T WORRY, I FEEL FINE!

MAYBE I SHOULD DRIVE...
NO, I'M DRIVING! I'M THE MAN AND THE MAN ALWAYS DRIVES! JUST YOU WATCH HOW GOOD I CAN DRIVE!

JERK!
SMASH!

THAT DOES IT... I'M CALLING A CAB...
NO, BUNNY, WAIT! I'M SOBER NOW! I'M SCARED STRAIGHT! I'LL DRIVE REAL SLOW! HONEST!

WELLL...IF YOU PROMISE TO DRIVE REAL SLOW... REMEMBER THAT WE'RE IN NO HURRY...
I PROMISE...AND I'LL STICK TO THE BACK ROADS...

LATER...
MAN, I COULDN'T WAIT TO GET OUT OF THERE... THOSE WOMEN WERE REALLY GETTING ON MY NERVES...
HOW SO?

WELL, THE HIGH POINT OF THE AFTERNOON WAS WHEN THEY ALL AGREED THAT ALL DRUG ADDICTS AND QUEERS SHOULD BE EXECUTED...
SERIOUSLY? DID YOU ARGUE WITH THEM?

NO. WHAT WOULD BE THE POINT OF THAT? THEY KNOW I DON'T AGREE... IT'S A CLOSED CASE AS FAR AS THEY'RE CONCERNED!
SHEESH... A BRIGADE OF FASCIST MOMMIES...

NO KIDDING...IT'S WEIRD HOW AS SOON AS PEOPLE START HAVING KIDS THEY BECOME CONVINCED THAT THE WOODS ARE CRAWLING WITH DOPE PEDDLERS AND SEX FIENDS JUST WAITING TO KIDNAP AND SODOMIZE THEIR CHILDREN...
YOU MEAN IT ISN'T TRUE?

VERY FUNNY... I JUST HOPE THAT I DON'T GET LIKE THAT IF I EVER HAVE A KID...
DON'T WORRY, YOU WILL...

THAT REMINDS ME, WALTER TOLD ME SOME PRETTY FUNNY HOMO JOKES — WANNA HEAR 'EM?
NO...WELL, OKAY, BUT ONLY IF THEY'RE FUNNY...

OKAY, WELL, THERE WERE THESE THREE HOMOS, SEE? AND....
HEH, HEH, HEH...

LATER, DOWNTOWN...
THE HIGH-FALOOTIN' FANCY-PANTS ART GALLERY
OPEN
THIS IS IT.
WAIT A MINUTE, LOOK AT THIS SIGN...

THIS IS A RADICAL FEMINIST ART SHOW! YOU DIDN'T TELL ME THAT!
BUT IT SAID SO RIGHT ON THE INVITATION! ARE YOU SAYING YOU DON'T WANT TO GO NOW?
SEXISM MUST DIE
A SEVEN WOMAN SHOW

NO, I'LL GO IN, AS LONG AS WE'RE HERE...
...I JUST HOPE THERE AREN'T ANY PICTURES OF GUYS GETTING THEIR DICKS CHOPPED OFF...
OH, DON'T BE RIDICULOUS!

BUNNY! I'M SO GLAD YOU CAME! I WAS AFRAID YOU WOULDN'T SHOW UP!
ARE YOU KIDDING? I WOULDN'T MISS YOUR SHOW FOR ANY- THING!
CHOP!
RIGHTEOUSNESS PREVAILS
I AM WOMAN
YIKES! I KNEW IT!

WANDA, YOU REMEMBER MY HUSBAND, CHET...
WHY, YES, HELLO...
BUNNY, I'M JUST DYING TO INTRODUCE YOU TO SOME OF THE OTHER WOMEN IN THE SHOW!
WILL YOU EXCUSE US FOR A MINUTE, CHET?
HUH? OH, SURE, I, UH...

YOU LOOK LIKE YOU'RE DRESSED FOR A PICNIC, BUNNY! IS THIS SOME SORT OF FASHION STATEMENT?
IT'S A LONG STORY... DON'T ASK...
HURUMPH! SEGREGATED AGAIN!

LATER...
CHET LEEWAY! FANCY MEETING YOU HERE! ...HEY, WHAT HAPPENED TO YOUR HEAD?
OH, HIYA PAUL... MY HEAD? OH... IT'S A LONG STORY... DON'T ASK...
I'M NOT ABOUT TO TELL THIS GUY I WAS PLAYING LAWN DARTS!
SISTERHOOD MARCHES

SO WHAT DO YOU THINK OF THE SHOW?
WELL, UH, TO TELL YOU THE TRUTH I DON'T THINK I'LL BE ABLE TO LOOK AT MUCH MORE OF IT BEFORE MY TESTICLES START TO RECEDE...
YEAH, I KNOW WHAT YOU MEAN. ...HEH HEH...

LIKE, CAN YOU BELIEVE THIS "PAINTING"? IT'S GOT "SOUR GRAPES" WRITTEN ALL OVER IT!
MY GIRLFRIEND DID THAT.
THIS IS MY LAST ATTEMPT AT GETTING MY WORK SHOWN IN THE MALE DOMINATED ART WORLD. PLEASE SUPPORT MY EFFORTS

YOUR GIRLFRIEND? GEE... I'M SORRY, I UH...
HEY, IT'S OKAY. IN FACT YOU'RE RIGHT! BUT SHE HAS GOOD REASON TO FEEL THAT WAY. WOMEN HAVE A REAL TOUGH TIME GETTING AHEAD IN THE ART WORLD.
IN FACT, SHE EVEN SLEPT WITH THE OWNER OF THIS GALLERY JUST TO INSURE THAT SHE'D BE IN- CLUDED IN THIS SHOW.

SHE DID?!? I MEAN, UH, ISN'T THAT KIND OF... HYPOCRITICAL?
WELL, NOT TOTALLY, SINCE THE OWNER IS A WOMAN. THAT'S HER OVER THERE, WITH THE LEGS...

OH, I SEE... (?!?)... AND, UM, THAT DOESN'T BOTHER YOU, THAT SHE, AND HER, UHH...
NO. WHY SHOULD IT? I'VE SLEPT WITH HER TOO, ONLY WITH ME IT WAS DIFFERENT, SINCE SHE WAS INTERESTED IN MY WORK FIRST, THEN TOOK AN INTEREST IN ME.
"ART EXPERTS"

OH, BUT OF COURSE!
SO TELL ME, IS THERE ANYONE ELSE IN THIS ROOM THAT YOU PORKED BUT DIDN'T HAVE TO TO HELP FURTHER YOUR CAREER?
HMM...LET'S SEE...OH, SEE THAT WOMAN OVER THERE WITH THE RED HAIR?
CHRIST, WHAT A BRAGGART!
JEALOUS

HMPH!
...SHE WRITES ART REVIEWS FOR ONE OF THE LOCAL PAPERS... I'VE BANGED HER QUITE A FEW TIMES...
SO THAT EXPLAINS ALL THOSE INEXPLICABLY POSITIVE REVIEWS YOU'VE RECEIVED...
BUT WHAT A HARD EXPRESSION SHE WEARS...I'M SUPRISED YOU WORKED UP THE NERVE TO EVEN APPROACH HER...

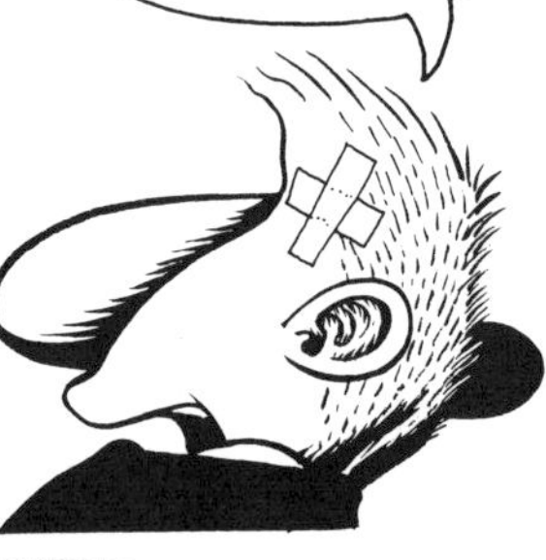

YEAH, WELL, SHE PUTS ON A TOUGH EXTERIOR TO HIDE THE FACT THAT SHE WANTS IT BAD—SHE'S REAL HORNY TONIGHT, I CAN TELL...
OH YEAH? WELL MAYBE THERE'LL BE ANOTHER GREAT "WRITE-UP" FOR YOU IN THE NEAR FUTURE! HEH-HEH...

HEY, HOW ABOUT THAT BALD GUY OVER THERE? HE LOOKS LIKE AN ART WORLD BIG SHOT—DID YOU EVER FUCK HIM?
THAT'S NOT FUNNY, CHET.

HEY, I WAS ONLY SPECULATING! AFTER ALL, IF YOUR GIRLFRIEND DOES IT...
THAT'S DIFFERENT. IT'S OKAY BETWEEN WOMEN, BUT GUYS—NO WAY.
I AIN'T NO FAGGOT, CHET.

OKAY, OKAY, WHO SAID YOU WERE? SHEESH!
MAN, THESE ARTIST-TYPES MAKE UP THE CRAZIEST RULES FOR THEMSELVES!
OOH, HEY, DIDJA SEE THAT GIRL THAT JUST WALKED BY IN THE WHITE DRESS? WELL...
NUDGE! NUDGE!

MEANWHILE...
SO THIS IS YOUR PIECE, WANDA? WHAT'S IT ALL ABOUT?
ISN'T IT OBVIOUS? IT'S AN ANTI-PORNOGRAPHY STATEMENT!
SHE DON'T PAINT TOO GOOD!

YOU SEE, THIS BIG HEAP IS MADE UP OF THE DISCARDED BODIES OF ABUSED WOMEN AND CHILDREN, WHILE UP ON TOP SITS A MAN WHO'S BEEN TRANS-FORMED INTO A RAGING BEAST WHILE READING HIS PORNO MAGAZINE.
I CALL IT "HEFNER'S LEGACY".
HUH. MY PARENTS USED TO SUB-SCRIBE TO PLAYBOY...
MAYBE THAT'S WHERE I GOT MY NAME FROM! YUK-YUK!

HMMM...Y'KNOW BUNNY, OUT OF ALL MY OLD FRIENDS I THOUGHT THAT AT LEAST YOU WOULD UNDER-STAND...
UNDERSTAND WHAT?

WHAT IT IS I'M TRYING TO SAY WITH MY WORK! AREN'T YOU EVEN AWARE OF HOW MEN MANIPULATE AND SUB-JUGATE US WOMEN?
WELL, YES, THAT IS, I'M AWARE OF HOW SOME MEN TRY TO MANIPULATE WOMEN, BUT...

SOME MEN? HA! IT'S THE WAY OUR WHOLE SOCIETY IS RUN, AND THE WAY IT ALWAYS HAS BEEN RUN!
LIKE, YOU WOULDN'T BELIEVE THE WAY WOMEN ARTISTS ARE TREATED BY THE PEOPLE WHO RUN THE ART BUSINESS, AND HOW THEY CUT US OFF FROM THE BIG MONEY...
WELL I KNOW THINGS HAVE BEEN ROUGH FOR YA, WANDA, BUT STILL, I THINK YOU'RE GENERAL-IZING A BIT MUCH...

OH, AM I? JUST THINK ABOUT THE WAY OUR OLD BOSS USED TO TREAT US! HE WOULDN'T HAVE TRIED TO GET AWAY WITH THAT STUFF IF WE WEREN'T WOMEN!
THAT'S BECAUSE WE QUIT!!
BUT HE DIDN'T "GET AWAY" WITH ANY-THING BECAUSE WE DIDN'T LET HIM!
THAT'S RIGHT! BUT I'VE HAD WOMEN BOSSES WHO WERE WORSE, SO WHAT'S THE DIFFERENCE?!

THE DIFFERENCE IS THAT MEN USE SEX AS A WEAPON! IT'S A WAY FOR THEM TO KEEP US AS 2nd CLASS CITIZENS! AND IT'S THE SAME WAY WITH RELA-TIONSHIPS, INCLUDING MARRIAGE!
NOT MY MARRIAGE!
ALL MARRIAGES!
HOW CAN YOU SAY THAT!

BECAUSE I KNOW! FOR THE LAST YEAR I'VE BEEN A PART OF A WOMEN ARTISTS' CO-OP, AND ONE OF THE BEST THINGS ABOUT IT IS THAT I CAN NOW LIVE MY LIFE WITHOUT HAVING TO DEAL WITH MEN AT ALL, AND I FINALLY FEEL LIKE I HAVE COMPLETE CONTROL OF MY OWN DESTINY...
SO WHAT ARE YOU SAY-ING, THAT YOU'RE A LESBIAN NOW?

SEX HAS NOTHING TO DO WITH IT! AND DON'T GO PINNING LABELS ON ME! ALL I'M TRYING TO DO IS FREE MYSELF FROM SOCIETY'S RESTRICTIONS...
BUT WHAT KIND OF FREEDOM IS THAT, GOING THROUGH LIFE AVOIDING MEN? YOU MIGHT AS WELL BECOME A NUN!
OH YEAH, SURE, AND WORSHIP JESUS, WHO'S A MAN! YOU SEE HOW THE SYSTEM WORKS? YOU SEE?!?
SIGH ALL I KNOW IS THAT FOR AS LONG AS I'VE KNOWN YOU YOU'VE BEEN STUCK ON THIS IDEA OF SEX-EQUALS-POWER, BUT YOU'VE BEEN AS GUILTY OF PERPETRATING IT AS ANY MAN HAS!
AND NOW YOU'RE TALKING LIKE A SPOIL SPORT BECAUSE YOU CAN'T WIN ALL THE TIME!
YOU WANNA TAKE YOUR BALL AND GO HOME!
THAT IS NOT THE WAY IT IS AT ALL, BUNNY! YOU OBVIOUSLY ARE UNABLE TO COMPREHEND WHAT IT IS I'M TALKING ABOUT!
WELL THEN WHY DON'T YOU TRY TO DO A BETTER JOB OF EXPLAINING IT TO ME?
I'D RATHER NOT WASTE MY TIME... NICE TALKING TO YOU, BUNNY.
YEAH, SAME HERE...
FRUSTRATED POWER-HUNGRY BITCH!
HOPELESS BRAINWASHED BIMBO!
LATER, IN THE STORAGE ROOM...
SO THERE YOU GUYS ARE! I WAS LOOKING ALL OVER FOR YOU!
WE'VE LOCATED THE SOURCE OF THE "FOLINARI SOAVE"!
WHERE ELSE WOULD WE BE?
SO, SOME SHOW, HUH? I TRUST WE'VE ALL LEARNED SOMETHING FROM IT...
YES, I'VE DEVELOPED A HEALTHY LOATHING OF MY OWN GENITALS. ...HOW ABOUT YOU, BUNNY?
OH, I'VE LEARNED THAT ALL OF MY GIRL-FRIENDS ARE ASSHOLES AND I HATE THEM ALL...
UH-HUH...AND IS THAT ALL?
...PLUS THAT IF I WAS A MAN I'D BE A WOMAN-BEATER...THAT'S ALL MOST OF 'EM DESERVE, ANYWAY...
HEY, WHAT'S ALL THIS STUFF?
THAT'S PART OF THE FOLK ART SHOW THAT'S GOING UP NEXT WEEK...
OOH! I LOVE THESE LITTLE DEVILS!
YEAH, THEY'RE COOL...SOME POOR OLD THIRD-WORLD PEASANT PROBABLY MASS-PRODUCES THEM FOR A BUCK EACH... I CAN JUST IMAGINE WHAT THIS PLACE WILL BE CHARGING FOR 'EM...
HEY! CHECK OUT THIS AFRICAN ART!

OH MY GOD!
NOW THIS IS WHAT I CALL ART!
IT'S GOT A MOVABLE PECKER!
IT'S NOT AFRICAN, IT'S POLYNESIAN. AND TAKE IT EASY WITH THAT THING, WILL YA CHET? JEEZ...
WANK! WANK!

BEND OVER, WENCH, AND YIELD TO THE POWER OF THE BIG BLACK PECKER GOD!
OH, YES, MASTER! "SUBJUGATE"* ME!
MAN, I CAN'T TAKE YOU GUYS ANYWHERE, 'CEPT FOR MAYBE THE ZOO!
UGH! UGH!
UGH!
* BUNNY LEARNS A NEW WORD FOR SEX
BUNNY LOOKS PRETTY CUTE IN THOSE SHORTS ...I WONDER IF THERE'S ANY CHANCE...

WHAT'S THAT SUPPOSED TO MEAN?
ARE YOU SAYING WE DON'T KNOW HOW TO ACT "COOL"?
WELL, YOUR BEHAVIOR IS HARDLY WHAT I'D CONSIDER TO BE "SOCIALLY ACCEPTABLE".

OH, I SEE, BUT THOSE PICTURES HANGING UP IN THAT GALLERY ARE "SOCIALLY ACCEPTABLE," AYE? THAT JUST GOES TO SHOW HOW FUCKED-UP SOME PEOPLE ARE!
YEAH, WE'RE JUST TRYING TO HAVE SOME FUN, BUT THERE SEEMS TO BE NO LIMIT TO HOW UPTIGHT SOME PEOPLE CAN BE...
HEY! WHOA! I'M NOT COMPLAINING! I'M IN FACT, DON'T EVER CHANGE! "I LOVE YOU JUST THE WAY YOU ARE"!
MR. NON-COMMITTAL

MAYBE WE SHOULD JUST GO HOME, BUNNY. THIS EVENING IS A LOST CAUSE...
I GUESS SO... BUT I DON'T WANT TO GO BACK OUT THERE AND FACE WANDA AGAIN...
YOU GUYS COULD ALWAYS SNEAK OUT THE BACK DOOR...

GOOD IDEA! THANKS PAUL!
YEAH, THANKS! SEE YA!
DON'T MENTION IT!
GOOD RIDDANCE!
EXIT

THAT PAUL AIN'T SUCH A BAD GUY, FOR A MALE PROSTITUTE...
BUT NOW WHERE ARE WE? MY SENSE OF DIRECTION IS ALL OFF NOW...

WE PARKED AROUND HERE SOMEWHERE...THAT WAY, I THINK...
SPARE CHANGE, MISTER?
GASP!

HEY, IT'S REAGAN'S FAULT!!! I MEAN, UH, IT'S GEORGE BUSH'S FAULT! GO HASSLE HIM, WHY DONTCHA!

...DRIVE HEADLONG INTO A GALLERY FULL OF HYPOCRITICAL, RE-PRESSIVE, MAN-HATING, SEX-HATING "RADICAL FEMINISTS"!!!
SO GO AHEAD, I WON'T STOP YOU.

WHAT, ARE YOU KIDDING? WE COULD GET ARRESTED! BUT IT'S FUN TO PRETEND, ISN'T IT?
...HEY, WHAT'S THE MATTER? YOU LOOK GLUM...
I'VE GOT THE BLUES...

CHET, DON'T YOU THINK IT'S PATHETIC THE WAY WE GO AROUND CRITICIZING EVERYBODY ALL OF THE TIME? LIKE, DON'T WE HAVE ANYTHING BETTER TO DO?
BUT THAT'S THE PRICE YA GOTTA PAY WHEN YOU TRY TO THINK FOR YOURSELF, AND EVERY-ONE AROUND YOU IS A GULLIBLE SAP WITH NO MIND OF THEIR OWN. AT LEAST WE DO A GOOD JOB OF TRASHING THESE PEOPLE, DON'T YOU AGREE?

BUT IS THAT ALL WE HAVE TO OFFER THE WORLD? IS THAT ALL WE'RE GOOD FOR?
WELLLL... IT'S BETTER THAN NOTHING...

YEAH... WELL, I'M ALSO FEELING BAD BECAUSE I DID A NAUGHTY THING...
UH-OH. WHAT DID YOU DO, SWEETUMS?

LOOK... I STOLE ONE OF THESE LIL' DEVIL GUYS...
WHY YOU LITTLE CRIMINAL, YOU!
THE DEVIL MADE ME DO IT! HEH-HEH...

SO WHERE ARE WE GOING TO DISPLAY THIS PIECE OF HOT MERCHANDISE?
I WAS THINKING OF GIVING IT AWAY AS A PRESENT...

A FEW DAYS LATER, IN A CERTAIN SUBURBAN MOBILE HOME...
HEY MA, LOOK AT WHAT CAME IN THE MAIL TODAY...
OH MY GOD! IT'S A WARNING FROM THE SATAN WORSHIP-PERS! WHERE'S YOUR BROTHER?
THEY MUST HAVE ABDUCTED HIM ALREADY!!!
HENRY! CALL THE POLICE!!!
THE END.

MISCELLANEOUS LOSERS

"WHY ME, OH LORD, WHY ME?"

THE SUFFERIN' BASTARD
WOE IS ME.

I WONDER WHAT HORRIBLE THINGS WILL HAPPEN TO ME TODAY?
I WONDER WHY I BOTHER GETTING OUT OF BED IN THE MORNING!
I SHUDDER TO THINK OF THE POS- SIBILITIES.
FATE HAS NEVER BEEN KIND TO ME.
RIGHT
WRONG

I FEEL POORLY THIS MORNING, AS USUAL...
...OH- NO!

...WHAT HIDEOUS, PAINFUL NEW DISEASE IS THIS?!?

I SHOULD HAVE KNOWN! IT'S AN INCUR- ABLE, 100% FATAL FORM OF CANCER!
THAT'S THE THIRTY- EIGHTH TERMINAL DISEASE I'VE CONTRACTED THIS WEEK!
RICHARD SCARY'S
BIG BOOK OF DISEASES

LATER...
NOW I'M LATE FOR MY APPOINTMENT AT THE UNEMPLOYMENT OFFICE!
IT'S JUST ONE MISFOR- TUNE AFTER ANOTHER!
I DON'T KNOW HOW I MANAGE TO SUR- VIVE FROM DAY TO DAY!...
BEEP! BEEP!

HAWAIIAN COCKTAIL HUMOR BY PETER BAGGE © 1986.

© 1987 BY PETER BAGGE

THE MANY MOODS AND MENTAL DISORDERS OF
ZOOVE GROOVER

ost people never would have ought that an illegal paraplegic ien with a speech impediment and n I.Q. of 43 would become the ottest act ever to come out of Menlo Park, New Jersey, since The Edison Lighthouse, but then again, most people aren't the Great Show-Biz Entrepreneur Sid Shyster! Said Sid: "The first time I saw Zoove I thought: 'Star Material!' I thought: 'Today's Youth!' I thought: 'Chart Action!' I thought 'Royalties!,' with a capital *R*!!!"

And just who is Zoove Groover? Two months ago, nobody could have answered that question, but now you could ask just about any teenager and not only could he tell you, but he could also slit your throat!!!

His music is hard to describe because it is so Now, so totally original, so incredibly "Zoova-phonic," as his Fans would say, that it can't be put into words, or even *to* words! Says Zoove: "My music is...well...garbage!" That's putting it mildly, Zoove!!!!! But you fans don't care what kind of music it is, do you, Fans? Ah, those loyal Fans, who bought 60 million copies of Zoove's first single, "Slap-Happy Holiday," and

who bought 35 million *Advanced Sale* copies of his current smash, "Havin' a Bong-a-Thon"'! Yes, the Fans who spend enough money in *One Week* to feed the *Whole World Ten Times Over!!!!!* I think that says something of the Greatness of Mr. Groover *and* his Fans!

This is not to say that Zoove doesn't have fans in High Places: Diana Ross has been quoted as saying that she considers Mr. Groover to be the most talented Human Being that ever lived; the President has presented him with the Medal of Honor; and the Pope Himself claims to have attended every date of Zoove's European tour! William F. Buckley said that Zoove has Literally redefined the meaning of the word "Cool;" Lou Rawls simply refers to him as "The Man;" and Frank Sinatra refers to him even more simply as "The."

So sit back, relax, crank up the Hi-Fi, and Groove to the Zoove!!!! After reading these liner notes you'll probably feel like you've got no choice!!!

— "Mad" Gene Bean
KBS - Seattle

SIDE ONE
SLAP-HAPPY HOLIDAY
(We're) HAVIN' A BONG-A-THON!
GRANNY'S OTHER PAD
WHY OH WHY OH WHY OH WHY OH SOB
ONION DIP

SIDE TWO
ZOOVE'S IN TOWN!
DO THE ZOOVE
LET'S ZOOVE AGAIN LIKE WE DID LAST SUMMER
I'M THE ZOOVE
MOODY ZOOVE (That's Me)
BIG NOISE FROM MENLO PARK (That's Me Too)

PRODUCED BY MURRAY WILSON
ENGINEER: J.R. Oppenheimer
MUSICIANS: Hal Blaine, Glen Campbell, Boots Randolph
GOFER: Sonny Bono

ALTHOUGH THIS RECORD IS RECORDED IN MONOPHONIC SOUND, WE GUARANTEE THAT IT CAN BE PLAYED ON ANY STEREOPHONIC SYSTEM. BE WARNED, HOWEVER, THAT IT MAY SOUND LIKE SHIT.

Anything is Possible

Those of you who know me may find it hard to imagine a pessimist such as myself uttering such a line, let alone believing it, but after witnessing the phenomenon—nay, miracle—that is the career of one Zoove "Mr. Amazing" Groover, I can say without a shadow of a doubt that anything and everything is possible! In just two and a half short years he has been more successful than any other entertainer in history, almost to the point where he now resides, all alone, in a yet-to-be defined Plateau of Greatness the likes of which no other performer—nay, Human—has ever or will ever approach. He has sold more records, done more T.V. appearances, sold out more concerts, turned down more product endorsements and borken more hearts in these two and a half mind-numbing years than the immortal Bing Crosby has in his entire career. His incredible string of 87 consecutive Number-One Hit Singles (move over, Joe Dimaggio) continues to grow, with the Swingin' "Havin' a Love Affair with Life" currently residing at the numero uno slot as of this writing. And perhaps the most historical achievement of all—and the one that means the most to Zoove himself—was when his beloved fellow citizens of his beloved home town of Menlo Park NJ officially proclaimed him their all-time greatest resident and favorite son (move over, Thomas Edison). One has to wonder what higher honor can be achieved after that (move over, George Washington)!

Yet the most amazing thing of all is that Zoove has done it all by simply being "the Zoove," and nothing else. He has outlasted all the dance-crazes, the surf-craze, the beatnik-craze, and the Go-Go-Craze without ever once trying to cash in on any of them, and its a sure bet that the Zoove will still be around long after this Limey "Mop-Top" craze has run its course. "After all," jokes Z.G., "I thought Female Impersonating went out with Milton Berle!" (No offense, Miltie—Zoove is one of your biggest fans!)

No sir, Mr. Groover will never sell out or try to jump on to any band-wagon other than the one he's on right now, and that's the one that's brought him right there to the top of the charts!

—Beaux Springley

GROOVER

ZOOVE GROOVER'S GOLDEN VAULT OF SOLID CLASSIC HITS! (VOL. VII)

GOLDEN VAULT OF LESS HITS (vol. VII)

SIDE 1

FEELIN' FREEWHEELIN'
AN' HIGH-FALOOTIN'

ITCHY PANTS!

ZOOMIN' WITH ZOOVE

I CAN'T GET NO) GRATIFICATION

STROKIN'

A TOWN WITHOUT PITY OR
PAYPHONES

SIDE 2

LOVE IS A GASSER

(HAVIN' A) LOVE AFFAIR WITH LIFE

STANDIN' ON THE SHAKEY
GROUND OF LOVE

WHO COMPILED THE DICTIONARY
OF LOVE?

ONLY THE YOUNG DIG LIFE

I'M SO YOUNG
(AND YOU'RE SO OLD)

A TRAGIC YET INSPIRING STORY AS
PERCEIVED THROUGH A SERIES OF
LINER-NOTES AND NEWS-CLIPPINGS
BY PETER BAGGE
© '86

ALL TITLES PRODUCED BY "BIGS" WHEELER IN COOPE-
RATION WITH SID SHYSTER ENTERPRISES. FOR FAN CLUB

Freaky First Side

LOVE vs. HATE (which side are you on?)
DON'T BUM ME OUT MR. BUSINESSMAN
ACID PLANET SUNDOWN
DON'T LET THE ESTABLISHMENT GIVE YOU A HEAVY
HAPPY BIRTHDAY, PISCES CHILD

Trippy Flip Side

THE THIRD UNIVERSE BEYOND ETERNITY
MY BIKE, MY BABE AND MY BONG ('Tis all I need)
MEDITATION: A NATURAL KIND OF HIGH
XPLGFRHNKSX
BAN HATE NOW (A CHANT)

BE FORWARNED. THIS IS NOT JUST AN ALBUM, IT'S A KALEIDOSCOPE. IT'S NOT JUST MADE TO BE HEARD, BUT ALSO TO BE SEEN, TO BE FELT AND TO BE SMELLED.

THE SOUNDS YOU'LL HEAR ARE COSMIC VIBRATIONS, THE LIKES OF WHICH HAVE NEVER BEFORE BEEN PERCEIVED BY MAN—SOUNDS THAT COME FROM THE OUTER-MOST REACHES OF THE GALAXY AND ARE REFLECTED THROUGH THE MIND OF ZOOVE GROOVER LIKE A PRISM (UNIVERSAL RECEPTOR). THE COLORS + LIGHTS YOU'LL SEE ARE THE FLASHING BRIGHT ORANGY CASCADES ONE WITNESSES WHILE IN DEEP MEDITATION DURING A SOLAR ECLIPSE (VISUAL MANTRA). THE FEELING YOU'LL EXPERIENCE IS THAT OF ZOOVE GROOVER'S BARED SOUL, TINGLING AND SQUIRMING IN YOUR HANDS (META PHYSICS), AND THE OVERPOWERING FRAGRANCE YOU'LL SMELL IS OF BURING INCENCE LONG FORGOTTEN FROM YOUR PAST LIVES (DEJA VU, REINCARNATION).

SINGER—SONGWRITER—PEACELOVER, ZOOVE GROOVER—ALONG WITH FELLOW POETS, DYLAN, LENNON, JAGGER AND MARK LINDSAY—HAVE BEEN PLACED ON THIS WAR-TORN PLANET BY HIGHER BEINGS IN ORDER TO ENLIGHTEN US, AND THIS 12 INCH OFFERING IS ZOOVE'S MOST IMPORTANT STATEMENT TO DATE, THE NEW SARGENT PEPPER. YOU WILL BE ACTING AS A MESSENGER OF PEACE AND LOVE SIMPLY BY BEING THE FIRST IN YOUR CROWD TO KNOW THIS, BUY THIS AND SHARE THIS ALBUM.
BE FOREWARNED.

ALL SONGS WRITTEN BY ZOOVE GROOVER
ARRANGED AND PRODUCED BY TERRY MELCHER
Thanks to all the Beautiful Cats and Gophers who helped contribute to the creation of this Vinyl Offering.

SIDE ONE
MY NAME IS MAHTAGURU
POSSESSIONS (I DO NOT NEED THEM)
HAMBURGERS = MURDER
SOME OF MY BEST FRIENDS ARE TREES
MAN vs. MACHINES (COMPUTER MADNESS)

SIDE TWO
POND-LIFE TRILOGY
PART 1: FISH
PART 2: AMPHIBIANS
PART 3: PLANKTON
NOURISHMENT SURROUNDS US (ODE TO EUELL GIBBONS)
SOLAR POWER (NOT NUCLEAR POWER)

"BIG BROWN", THE HOME OF MAHTAGURU'S COMMUNE AND WHERE THIS ALBUM WAS RECORDED.

A MESSAGE FROM MAHTAGURU:

IT HAS TAKEN ME NEARLY TWO YEARS TO COMPOSE AND RECORD THIS ALBUM, AND ANOTHER TWO YEARS OF HASSLING WITH ALL THE GREEDY, MATERIALISTIC, NATURAL-RESOURCE-RAPING RECORD COMPANIES WHO ALL REFUSED TO AGREE TO MY DEMANDS, SUCH AS ONLY USING RECYCLED PAPER, INK AND VINYL IN THE MANUFACTURE OF THIS ALBUM, PLUS NO ADVERTISING OR PROMOTION OF ANY KIND IN ORDER TO AVOID HAVING MY WORK MISINTERPRETED AND PURCHASED BY THE WRONG PEOPLE FOR THE WRONG REASONS (I HAVE FAITH THAT THE RIGHT PEOPLE WILL BE ABLE TO FIND THIS RECORD THROUGH DEVINE GUIDANCE). DESPITE ALL THESE OBSTACLES THAT STOOD IN THE WAY OF MY PROJECT, I HAVE NEVER ONCE WAVERED IN MY DETERMINATION TO SEE IT THROUGH, FOR I CONSIDER THIS ALBUM TO BE MY REDEMPTION, MY WAY OF ASKING FORGIVENESS FOR MY PAST ERRORS FROM THE POWERS THAT BE, AND TO RECONCILE MYSELF WITH THE ONENESS OF NATURE. TO THOSE OF YOU STILL LIVING IN THE CAPITALISTIC MACHINE WORLD AND DO NOT DESIRE TO LEAVE IT, I HAVE NOTHING TO SAY. NOR DO I CONDEMN YOU, FOR YOU ARE ALREADY LIVING IN YOUR OWN HELL. BUT TO THOSE OF YOU WHO ALSO FEEL THE NEED FOR REDEMPTION AND WHO FEEL THE POWER OF NATURE'S PRESENCE ON THIS ALBUM, YOU ARE WELCOME TO JOIN ME AT MY COMMUNE HERE IN THE ROCKY MOUNTAINS (ADDRESS IS GIVEN IN ONE OF THE SONGS), OR TO START A COMMUNE OF YOUR OWN. AS MY PERSONAL GURU, THE WISE + HOLY HINDUBUDDASHINTO FELDSTEIN, ALWAYS SAYS: "A THING OF BEAUTY IS A JOY FOREVER," AND THIS APPLIES TO ALL OF YOU WHO HEEDS MY MESSAGE AND JOINS ME IN MY ALL-NATURAL WAY OF LIFE.
— Z. MAHTAGURU G.

THIS ALBUM WAS WRITTEN, PRODUCED, ENGINEERED AND PERFORMED ENTIRELY BY MYSELF. THIS IS NOT BECAUSE I'M ON SOME KIND OF EGO TRIP, BUT SIMPLY BECAUSE I DID NOT WANT ANYONE TO DISTRACT ME FROM MY PERSONAL VISION.

HOMESPUN RECORDS

"HOMESPUN RECORDS IS THE NAME OF MY LABEL, BUT IT IS NOT COPYRIGHTED BECAUSE PROPERTY IS A SIN. HELL, IT'S JUST A GODDAMNED NAME, MAN! GO AHEAD AND RIP ME OFF, I DON'T CARE. IT'S YOUR KARMA YOU..."

EX-POP SINGER ARRESTED

Charged with Vandalism and Destruction of Livestock. More Charges May Follow.

By B. SPRINGLEY, Jr.
Staff Reporter

JERKWATER, CO.—Former '60s Pop Singer and Teen Idol Zoove "Mahtaguru" Groover was arrested and brought into custody by today by Jerkwater police on a number of charges ranging from disturbing the peace to the random slaughter of neighboring rancher's livestock. He may also face charges of bigamy, brought on by an ex-wife who claims they were never divorced, as well as income tax evasion and for growing marijuana with intent to sell. Law enforcement agencies are still investigating these charges.

Today's arrest could be the culmination of a long and tragic fall from grace for Groover (born: Zachary Groover, in Menlo Park, N.J., 1943), who enjoyed considerable success as a recording artist for a few short years in the mid-sixties. But by 1966 his star began to fall just as quickly as it had risen, and by 1967 his record sales were disasterous.

Groover's career all but come to an end in 1969 when he was dropped by his long-time manager Sid Shyster (who is currently serving a prison sentence for racketeering and fraud), a move that was marked by bitter feelings and violent arguments. Since then Groover has been unsuccessful in finding anyone to agree to manage him or give him a record contract, this being due not only to lack of public interest, but also because of his notoriously huge ego and wild, unpredictable personality.

In 1972 Groover himself financed his one last album "Air, Water and Dirt," which proved to be an unprecedented flop. Anticipating huge sales, Groover reportedly printed up 200,000 copies, only to sell roughly 300 copies, and Groover was forced to file for bankrupcy. This failure, coupled with the death of his one-time colleague Bobby Darin, seemed to be too much for the already unstable Groover, in that his behavior from this point on became extremely erratic and unexplainable. He had

Zoove "Mahtaguru" Groover is accompanied by a girlfriend as he's brought into the county jail.

by this time adopted the pseudo-eastern philosophies of a guru named Hindubuddashinto Feldstein—a former chemistry teacher of Groover's—and began calling himself "Mahtaguru." He divorced his first wife, quickly married and divorced a second, and had started a commune here in northwest Colorado. Members of the commune changed constantly over the last three years, but at the time of his arrest was living with a third wife, two girlfriends and a brood of legitimate and illegitimate children, whose estimated numbers ranged anywhere from seven to thirty-three.

Groover had been at odds with both his neighbors and the law from the moment he established his Rocky Mountain commune. At first the locals complained about the noisy wild goings-on at the commune, which semed to be a stop-off point for every freak and weirdo travelling cross-country. Shortly after that he began harassing the locals, confronting them on the streets and at their homes with his political and religious beliefs. A strict vegetarian, he would accuse local ranchers of being "mass-murderers," and would often try to talk the area's young people into joining his commune, without much success. "He used to bug me and my sister all the time," says one 15 year old girl who lived nearby. "He wanted us to leave our parents and move in with him. I couldn't imagine anything more gross." "A lot of what he said made sense," said another local high-school girl. "He had some really beautiful ideas. It's just too bad he smelled so awful."

Things finally came to a head three months ago, when nearby ranchers started finding a number of their sheep were being brutally mutilated in the middle of the night, and of sometimes finding slogans like "Death to Nazi Pigs" written in huge letters with blood on the sides of their barns. It didn't take long for the local authorities to positively link the crimes with Groover's commune, though further evidence suggests that Groover may have acted alone in these crimes.

Once under arrest, Groover readily admitted to the crimes, his excuse being that he wanted the animals to die "with their Karma intact, and not to have their remains consumed by humans." But later on he became more regretful for his actions, and explained to one reporter that "Nothing's been the same since Bobby (Darin) died."

No charges have been brought against the commune women as of yet, and at the time of his arrest they were angrily voicing his innocence. "I bought my first Zoove Groover record in 1963," said one girlfriend. "I thought he was God then and I still think he's God." "He's not God," said the other, "he's better than God." But after learning of his confession, both girlfriends have agreed to testify against him, and his wife intends to file for a divorce.

Meanwhile, the entire community of Jerkwater are quite incensed over this whole affair, and are demanding to see justice done in the case of "Mahtaguru" Groover. Said one rancher, "I just hope they do to him what he had done to my sheep, and see how his Karma feels about that!"

EX-MANAGER: "HE'S INSANE"

ASSOCIATED PRESS

Zoove Groover's former manager Sid Shyster spoke to reporters today about Groover's arrest at Leavenworth Penitentiary, where Shyster is serving a 10-15 year sentence for numerous counts of fraud and racketeering charges.

"I'm not at all surprised by this," said Shyster upon hearing the news, and feels Groover should have been "put away years ago. The man is a raving lunatic."

When asked how a one-time teen idol could have sunk this far, Shyster claimed that Groover's short-lived success was based solely on "hype, and of my pulling a few strings within the music business.

"All that talk about 'Zoovmania' in the mid-sixties was totally pre-fabricated. His records sold well at first, but once he started slipping, we began billing him as America's answer to the Beatles, and as the New Bobby Darin, anything to fool the public into buying his records.

"Of course it didn't work for the simple reason that Bobby Darin and the Beatles had some talent, while Zoove—or should I say "Mahtaguru"—Groover doesn't have a talented bone in his body. Unfortunately, the only person who did believe our press-releases was Zoove himself."

Shyster dropped Groover in 1969, from which point on Groove would frequently harass and threaten him. "He blamed me for everything from his income tax problems to the Vietnam War. It was quite obvious that the man was losing his mind, so I tried to avoid him as much as I could.

"Now I realize how close I could've come to getting killed. Guess I'm lucky I've been in jail the last few years, huh?"

Below: Shyster talks to reporters at Leavenworth.

ROCK SINGER RELEASED
FROM MENTAL INSTITUTION

DENVER (UPI)—1960s rock star Zoove Groover was released from a high security mental institution today after residing for four years for a number of criminal offenses—including the killing of sheep—for which he was ruled insane.

Arrested for these crimes in late 1975, Groover was facing a possible five to ten year prison sentence as well as stand trial for other charges, but a jury found him innocent by reason of insanity, and a judge ruled that Groover be placed in an institution for the criminally insane for a minimum of 10 years.

Thanks to the intervention of Groover's ex-wife, Melinda Cartwheel (of the wealthy Cartwheel family of Dallas, Texas) the State re-examined his case and agreed to release Groover in the custody of the Cartwheel family. Evidently Groover has shown a remarkable improvement, though hospital officials still refuse to give him a clean bill of health, and Groover must report to a local Dallas mental facility once a week, where his behavior will be closely monitored.

Groove divorced Ms. Cartwheel—his first of three wives—in 1970, but they have been in close contact since he's been committed, and she has given him both emotional and financial support during his stay at the institution. All parties seem to attribute his recovery to her constant support as well as to his renewed faith in Christianity, which she also encourages.

ZOOVE GROOVER

After years of failure, tragedy and mental illness, the legendary '60s rock singer is back in the groove

by Beverley Springley-Mudd

It's hard for me to believe that this happy, healthy, respectable-looking middle-aged man standing before me outside the suburban Dallas Baptist church is the once-famous—and once-infamous—Zoove Groover. Unable to conceal my amazement, Groover gave me a knowing smile and said that if he were me he'd be just as startled, "although my faith and belief in God has taught me that anything is possible. What you see standing before you is a modern-day miracle."

Regardless of how much of a "believer" you may be, anyone would agree that this ex-pop-singer/criminal/mental-patient's return to grace is quite a remarkable story, if not a full-blown miracle. Twenty years ago, Zoove Groover (born Zach Grover in 1943) was at the top of the pop music industry. His live act was a top draw both in Vegas and in the concert halls, he was a familiar face on all the variety and teen-dance T.V. shows, and his recording out-put from 1963 to 1966 was enormous. Despite their admittedly dubious quality, his records sales were also enormous, thanks mostly to relentless publicity and the sharp business mind of his manager, the late Sid Shyster.

But by the late sixties Groover's image seemed outdated, and his record sales began to slip. From that point on one disaster lead to another, and by 1970 his career seemed finished. "Looking back I realize I brought it all on myself" recalls Zoove." I was used to all that money and fame, and I couldn't imagine living without it, so I became a panicky, paranoid monster." Nearly everyone associated with Groover broke their ties with him by this time, and Zoove found himself without a friend in the industry, "I accused everyone of deserting me, when actually I drove them all away with my gigantic wounded ego raging out of control. Then I made the biggest mistake of my life by driving Melinda away," Melinda being Zoove's first and once-again current wife (they were re-married in 1980.) Zoove met Mrs. Groover, born Melinda Cartwheel, heiress to the Cartwheel oil empire, in 1965 when he was guest on the Jerry

Zoove Groover with wife Melinda Cartwheel-Groover, whom he's been married to twice: "Thank God for second chances."

Lewis telethon and she was doing volunteer work for the M.S. association. Her family was dead set against her marrying him, and this pressure, coupled with Zoove's emotional problems and explosive temper, eventually lead to her reluctantly agreeing to a divorce.

Without his supportive wife or any kind of career, Zoove began leading a crazed counter-culture existance on a Colorado commune, living with a long succession of wives and girlfriends. He began turning to drugs and eastern philosophies for an answer to his miserable existence, but wound up being only more lost and confused. "I would've never admitted it at the time, but I was still caught up in the materialistic world, pursuing cheap thrills," reflects Zoove. "I was continually being led astray by the devil."

Then came all the senseless, heavily publicized crimes, which landed Zoove in a home for the criminally insane for four years. As open as Zoove is about his past, he's still very reluctant to talk about that particular episode, saying it would only serve as an embarrassment to all concerned. "I'm still trying to pay people back for all the harm I've done, and it would only make matters worse by bringing it all up again." But when I asked him about the charge brought against him by an ex-wife, claiming they were never legally divorced, he said "It turns out we were never legally married. I never even knew what her name was, that's how out-of-it I was at

the time."

Throughout all these crazy years, Melinda felt she knew he would "see the light" and that they'd get back together. It turned out that it was Melinda herself that lead Zoove to that light. They came in contact again while he was in the mental hospital, where she began visiting him on a regular basis. Alone, broke and manic-depressive, Zoove cherished Melinda's company and support as being the only things that gave him any kind of hope for a future, and it was through her brave, tireless efforts that he was released from the nightmarish facility and placed into her family's custody. A devout Baptist family, the elder Cartwheel consented to their re-marriage and agreed to accept Zoove into their family once they saw that he had finally accepted Christ as his Savior. "it wasn't an act of charity on my family's part, says Melinda, "Just a simple case of helping someone who wants to help himself."

Married once again—and happily this time—Zoove is now working for his Father-in-law's corporation, and is active in local church activities. He also is thinking of starting up a singing career again, though he's very tentative about how he'll go for it. "I won't be doing it for the money or ego-fulfillment this time," says Zoove. "I want my music to serve as a message, to help young people avoid the same traps that I had fallen into. I want them to know that there is an answer to life's problems, and that answer is God."

<u>FOR IMMEDIATE RELEASE</u>

Contact: Beaux Springley III
Publicity Dept. -- MM/VE
Release date: July 1986

Z O O V E   G R O O V E R   R E L E A S E S
C O M E B A C K   L. P.,   V I D E O

Scheduled for release this summer is "Friends in High Places," the first Album by famed '60s rock star Zoove Groover in fourteen years. Also due out this summer is "Dead End Street," the first single and video to be culled from the L.P. The video will debut on the Christian Broadcasting Network on July 13th.

Both the L.P. and the video have already been the subject of controversy, partly because of Groover's refusal to work with any musicians, technicians or actors who aren't Born-Again Christians, and also due to the video's explicit display of sex, violence and drug use, which seems to be contradictory to Groover's religious beliefs. Yet Groover claims the video has a strong religious message, and explains: "I want to grab young people's attention by showing the dangerous things that appeal to their weaknesses, like sexy, worldly women, fast cars, drugs, etc. By vividly showing these drug-crazed prostitutes smashing full speed into a stone wall in their Jaguar convertible I'll be driving home the message that this is what these things lead to: A dead end street and an early grave."

Zoove Groover today.

Groover's tragic, sordid life history has been well documented, yet his remarkable recovery and current involvement in worthy causes should be even more newsworthy, for he not only is a figure of inspiration to his own "baby-boomer" generation, but can serve as an excellent example to today's troubled young people. His new recording should be given a lot of attention, if only as a tribute to this brave man, one of the giants of Rock & Roll history.

-- 30 --

...THERE'S A WORLD WHERE I CAN GO AND TELL MY SECRETS TOOOOOO...
♫ IN MY ♫ ROOM...
©1985 PETER BAGGE
ATLAS SHRUGGED
DRUNK DRIV AGAINST MO
I HATE THIS SONG.

RRRIIINNNGGG!
UGH.
..SOLID GOLD ROCK 'N' ROLL!

HELLO?... ..OH, HI, WHAT'S UP... ..WHAT THING TONIGHT?.. ..OH YEAH, I FORGOT... YES, I'M GOING... I SAID I'D GO, DIDN'T I?..
...HEY JIM, DIDJA GET A HOLD OF THAT JAYNE MANSFIELD VIDEO TAPE?..OF COURSE I MEAN THE UNCUT VERSION!... NO, HUH?.. THAT FIGURES...
...TODAY'S TRIVIA QUESTION IS: WHO WAS THE ONLY DANISH INSTRUMENTALIST TO HAVE MORE THAN ONE TOP 20 U.S. HIT IN THE SAME YEAR?..
BROTHER THEODORE

..SO WHAT ARE YOU GOING TO BE SHOWING TONIGHT?..'BEANIE AND CECIL'!? I'VE SEEN ALL THOSE...YEAH, I SUPPOSE I COULD STAND WATCHING THEM AGAIN...
...WHO ELSE IS GONNA BE THERE?...OH, HIM, EH?..NO, I DON'T CARE, SO LONG AS HE DOESN'T START TALKING ABOUT GEORGE STEINBRENNER...YEAH, I'M SURE IT'LL BE FUN.. SEE YA...
...VICTOR BORGE? THAT ANSWER IS... INCORRECT!

...A GODDAMN MORON CONVENTION IS WHAT IT'S GONNA BE!
...THIS NEXT SONG IS FOR ALL YOU FOLKS IN REDMOND...

OH NO! NOT THIS SONG!!
...PEOPLE... PEOPLE WHO NEED PEOPLE...

HUH. DISCO. GUESS I'LL LISTEN TO THIS FOR AWHILE...
...CHAKA KAHN CHACKA KAHN LEMMIE ROCK YA CHAKA KAHN CHAKA, UH DO YA FEEL FO' ME THE WAY I FEEL FO' YOU UH CHAKA?...
DRUNK DRIVE AGAINST MATH

ITCH! ITCH!
YOO ARE MY FAN-TUH-SEE, BAY-BUH...
YAWWNN
SCRATCH! SCRATCH!

PEE-YOO! I STINK!
...I WANT COFFEE...
NER EVERYBODY STAHT BRAY-KIN!

GOOD. THERE'S STILL SOME LEFT FROM YESTERDAY.
...JEEZ! I LEFT THIS THING ON ALL NIGHT! COULDA STARTED A FIRE...
...I OUGHTA WATCH OUT FOR THINGS LIKE THAT.
SNIFF! SNIFF! JUST THE RIGHT AMOUNT BURNT!

WHAT'S THIS?...
TONY'S PIZZA

LUNCH
YOU'VE TRIED ALL THE REST -
NOW TRY THE BEST!

UGH! I'VE HAD IT WITH THESE LOUSY RADIO STATIONS!
...WAR IS STOO-PID! WAR IS STOO-PID!...
CLICK!

IT'S TIME FOR SCOOBIE-DOO ANY-WAY...
CLICK!

TONIGHT'S EIGHT O'CLOCK MOVIE IS "TEACHER'S PET", STARRING DORIS DAY...
TEACHER'S PET! I HAVEN'T SEEN THAT MOVIE IN... MONTHS!
AND I'VE GOTTA MISS IT! SHIT!

I SHOULD GET READY TO GO OUT BEFORE I START GETTING TOO COMFORTABLE.
...SCOOBIE DOOBIE DOO, WHERE ARE YOU, SCOOBIE DOOBIE DOO WHERE ARE YA?!...
SHIT.

ARRGH! IT'S TOO SUNNY OUT!
A GUY COULD GO BLIND OUT THERE...
...C'MON SCOOBIE! THERE'S NOTHING TO BE AFRAID OFF!

PEE-YOO! THESE SHIRTS STINK!
I GUESS I'LL JUST WEAR THE ONE I HAVE ON...

OUCH! THE COMB BROKE IN MY HAIR...
AND NOW I CAN'T GET THE BROKEN PIECES OUT! GREAT!

AH, FORGET IT! WHERE'S MY SHOES?!
THERE'S ONE...

NUKE THE WHALE
ALRIGHT, NOW WHERE'S THE OTHER SHOE?!?

HOW AM I GOING TO FIND ANYTHING IN THIS PIG-STY!?
SHIT!

...THIS ROOM IS A GOD-DAMNED DISASTER AREA...
...HEY, WHAT'S THIS?!...
ROCK+ROLL M-S

WOW! IT'S THAT ISSUE OF FANFARE MAGAZINE I HAD LOST BEFORE I EVER HAD THE CHANCE TO READ IT!
AND IT WAS THREE FEET AWAY FROM ME THE WHOLE TIME!
Fanfare

"...THE MOVIE POSTER ART OF FRANK FRAZETTA"...
MAN, THERE'S SOME GREAT STUFF IN HERE...
THIS IS LIKE FINDING BURIED TREASURE!

HELLO, JIM?... LISTEN, I CAN'T COME OVER TONIGHT, SOMETHING CAME UP... NO I'M NOT LYING! I'LL TELL YOU ABOUT IT LATER...
...BY THE WAY, I FOUND THAT COPY OF FANFARE... YEAH... SO I'M SORRY I ACCUSED YOU OF STEALING IT...
...YEAH, RIGHT... SOME OTHER TIME THEN... SEE YA.

...TEACHER'S PET, I WANNA BE TEACHER'S PET...
MAN, FRANK FRAZETTA IS A GENIUS!
DRUNK DRIVERS AGAINST MOTHERS

I LIKE TO THINK I'M SMART, BUT THEN I THINK, IF I'M SO SMART, WHY AM I ALWAYS SO MISERABLE? IF I WAS SMART, WOULDN'T I FIGURE OUT A WAY TO BE HAPPY? I MUST BE DUMB TO EVEN WASTE MY TIME THINKING OF DOPEY STUFF LIKE THIS? DO YOU THINK IT'S DUMB? DO YOU THINK I'M DUMB?

I KNOW THAT MOST PEOPLE THINK I'M CRAZY. PROBABLY BECAUSE I ALWAYS SAY WHAT I THINK. I ALWAYS HAVE TO SAY WHATEVER POPS INTO MY HEAD. BUT I LIKE TO EXPRESS MY THOUGHTS, I LIKE TO "RELATE". I HATE TO THINK THAT I'M THE ONLY PERSON THAT THINKS THE THINGS THAT I THINK. DOES THAT MAKE SENSE TO YOU?

THE BIGGEST HIGH FOR ME IS A REAL GOOD, REAL INTENSE BOOK. SOMETIMES A BOOK WILL AFFECT ME SO DEEPLY, LIKE IT WAS WRITTEN ABOUT ME IN A DIFFERENT TIME ZONE OR SOMETHING. SOMETIMES I'LL READ A BOOK THAT WILL MAKE ME THINK OH MY GOD! EVERYTHING I KNOW IS WRONG! EVERYTHING! Y'KNOW? AND THEN I HAVE TO FIGURE OUT LIFE ALL OVER AGAIN...

SOMETIMES I THINK I'M GOING CRAZY,

AND OTHER TIMES I THINK I'M THE ONLY SANE PERSON ON EARTH, AND THAT EVERYONE ELSE IS CRAZY. DO YOU EVER FEEL THAT WAY? DO YOU EVER FEEL LIKE YOU'RE LOSING YOUR GRIP ON REALITY? I FEEL THAT WAY ALL THE TIME.

I HATE PARTIES. I HATE TO SMOKE POT. WHEN I GET STONED I HAVE TO DESCRIBE EVERYTHING I THINK AND FEEL. I HAVE TO KNOW THAT EVERYONE IS THINK-ING AND FEELING THE SAME THINGS. AND IF SOME-ONE DOESN'T KNOW WHAT I'M TALKING ABOUT I GET REALLY SCARED. I FREAK OUT! UGGH, I HATE THAT!

©1984 by PETER BAGGE
WELL OKAY, I GUESS I LIKE SHLOCKY COMMERCIAL STUFF SOMETIMES TOO. SOMETIMES I GET TIRED OF BEING A GRUNGY BOHEMIAN ALL THE TIME, LIVING ALL ALONE IN MY CRUMMY APARTMENT, SO I LIKE TO WATCH DOPEY SHOWS LIKE "THE LOVE BOAT" AND EAT HOSTESS CUPCAKES AND PRETEND I'M A LITTLE KID IN MY PARENTS HOUSE IN THE SUBURBS AGAIN. C'MON, ADMIT IT, YOU GET THAT WAY TOO SOMETIMES, DON'T YOU?
...WHO CAN TURN THE WORLD ON WITH HER SMILE...
THIS PROBABLY SOUNDS HORRIBLE, BUT I ALWAYS THINK ABOUT KILLING MYSELF. ONCE I WAS PLANNING ON PULLING OFF A FAKE SUICIDE, JUST TO SEE WHAT PEOPLE WOULD SAY ABOUT ME IF THEY THOUGHT I WAS DEAD. THAT'S THE ONLY TIME PEOPLE WILL EVER SAY WHAT THEY REALLY THINK ABOUT YOU, IS AFTER YOUR DEAD. DON'T YOU THINK SO? HMM? OH, MAYBE I'M WRONG. MAYBE I'M JUST PLAIN NUTS...
MY LITTLE BROTHER IS MORE LIKE ME, I THINK, THOUGH HE DOESN'T WANT TO ADMIT IT. HE LISTENS TO THAT AWFUL HEAVY METAL MUSIC, DON'T ASK ME WHY. WELL, MAYBE HE FEELS LIKE HE'S SUPPOSED TO LIKE IT, AND HE'S JUST TRYING TO FIT IN. I KNOW HOW HORRIBLE THAT CAN BE, TRYING TO BE ACCEPTED. I TRY TO TALK TO HIM ABOUT IT, BUT HE ALWAYS TELLS ME TO GET LOST.
BANG HE HEAD F THOSE O DO
MY BIGGEST HEROES IN LIFE ARE MASS MURDERERS, LIKE CHARLIE MANSON AND RICHARD SPECK. IT'S NOT THAT I WANT TO BE A MURDERER TOO—I CAN'T EVEN KILL A COCKROACH. MAYBE THAT'S WHY I ADMIRE THEM, BECAUSE THEY CAN BRING THEMSELVES INTO DOING SUCH AN UNTHINKABLE ACT, SOMETHING SO OUTRAGEOUS THAT THEIR REASONS FOR DOING IT BECOME INCONSEQUENTIAL. WHO NEEDS A REASON FOR DOING ANYTHING?
HELTER SKELTER
MANSON #1

MY SISTER AND I ARE EXACT OPPOSITES. WHENEVER I TRY TO RELATE TO HER OR EVEN TRY TO HAVE A REGULAR PLAIN OL' CONVERSATION WITH HER SHE JUST GRUNTS AND DRIVES OFF TO THE MALL. SHE ONLY BUYS TOP 40 RECORDS AND WEARS WHAT EVERY BODY ELSE WEARS. I GUESS THAT'S WHY I ALWAYS LIKED REALLY WEIRD AND DIFFERENT STUFF, IS BECAUSE I DON'T WANT TO BE LIKE HER. I GUESS I HATE HER. DOES THAT SOUND BAD?
I HATE SUNDAYS

I NEVER HAVE A STEADY BOYFRIEND FOR VERY LONG. I THINK SOME GUYS LIKE ME AT FIRST 'CUZ I'M WEIRD, BUT THEN THEY WIND UP HATING ME 'CUZ I'M TOO WEIRD. SOMETIMES I THINK I ACT WEIRDER THAN I REALLY AM, JUST TO SEE HOW THEY'LL TAKE IT. IT'S KIND OF LIKE A "TEST". JEEZ, WHEN I THINK OF SOME OF THE THINGS I'VE DONE, IT'S NO WONDER THEY ALWAYS HEAD FOR THE HILLS!
...I DON'T KNOW WHAT'S WRONG WITH HER! SHE'S JUST BEEN SITTING THERE GRITTING HER TEETH FOR HOURS...LOOK, I'VE GOT TO GET OUT OF HERE...

THANKS TO STEPHANI K.

WARNING: THE NARRATOR OF THIS STORY HAS A TENDENCY TO EXAGGERATE, SO AN ASTERISK(*) HAS BEEN PLACED AT EACH SUCH INSTANCE IN ORDER TO PROTECT THE READER FROM ANY MISINFORMATION.

THE REJECT.

© 1984 BY P. BAGGE - THANKS TO GEORGE "CHEAPMEAT" PACCIELLO, FATHER OF THE CHINESE GRASS TORTURE.

I'M SURE YOU'VE ALL KNOWN SOME REAL JERKS IN YOUR LIFE, BUT I KNEW A KID THAT WAS SUCH A REJECT THAT I DON'T EVEN WANNA TALK ABOUT IT..... BUT I WILL ANYWAY, BECAUSE MAYBE IF YOU EVER START FEELING SORRY FOR YOURSELF YOU COULD THINK ABOUT THIS KID AND REALIZE THAT YOU COULD BE ALOT WORSE OFF!

JORGIE JOHANSEN. THAT WAS HIS NAME. AND THE J's WERE PRONOUNCED LIKE Y's. WEIRD KID, WEIRD NAME.

HE WAS REAL STUPID LOOKING, WITH THESE FROG-EYES AND A STUPID HAIR-CUT. AND HE SLOUCHED. AND HE SLOBBERED. AND HE ALWAYS HAD HIS STUPID SKI-CAP ON. ALWAYS.*

THIS KID WAS A WRECK. HE WAS REAL SKINNY, BUT HAD A BLOATED STOMACH LIKE A BIAFRAN. HE ALWAYS HAD DRIED SNOT ON HIS STUFFED-UP NOSE AND HAD TO BREATHE THROUGH HIS MOUTH.

HE MIGHT'VE HAD A SERIOUS HEALTH PROBLEM, BUT IF HE **DID** IT WAS HIS **OWN FAULT**, BECAUSE HE NEVER PLAYED SPORTS AND HE ATE **LOUSY, DISGUSTING, UNNUTRITIOUS** FOOD.

HIS FAVORITE THING TO DO WAS TO STAND IN HIS FRONT YARD AND IDENTIFY CARS AS THEY DROVE BY, WHILE HE SNACKED ON ONE OF HIS **KETCHUP** SANDWICHES.

ANYWAY, HE WAS A **REAL JERK.** AND HE **SMELLED.***

THE BUS WAS THE REJECT'S TORTURE CHAMBER. EVERY DAY WE'D GIVE HIM **HELL.**

HIS ONLY CHANCE FOR SURVIVAL WAS TO SIT BEHIND THE BUS DRIVER, WHO SAVED HIS LIFE A COUPLE OF TIMES.*

HE WAS THE ONLY KID ON THE BUS THAT WOULD GET PICKED ON, FOR SOME REASON. WELL, WE DIDN'T HAVE ANY **CRIPPLES** OR **MINORITIES** ON OUR ROUTE, SO I GUESS HE WAS ALL WE HAD.

MY FRIEND **JOEY LARSON** REALLY HAD IT IN FOR THE REJECT. HE WOULD PICK ON HIM **NON-STOP**, ALWAYS TRYING TO GET A REACTION OUT OF HIM, BUT THE REJECT WOULD JUST IGNORE HIM AND STARE INTO SPACE, WHICH WOULD MAKE JOEY GET ON HIS CASE EVEN **WORSE.**

JOEY WAS MY BEST FRIEND* BUT HE COULD BE A **REAL BASTARD.** WHEN HE MOVED AWAY I WAS KINDA GLAD, BECAUSE I THINK HE WAS SLIGHTLY **PSYCHO.**

ANYHOW, JUST TO PROVE TO YOU WHAT A **REJECT** THE REJECT WAS, LET ME TELL YOU ABOUT THIS GIRL THAT ALWAYS SAT BEHIND HIM ON THE BUS.

HER NAME WAS **KATIE KUNKEL**, AND SHE WAS A REJECT TOO, BUT A DIFFERENT KIND: SHE DIDN'T TALK TO **YOU** AND NO ONE TALKED TO **HER**. AND I THINK SHE WAS SUPPOSED TO BE REAL SMART.

WELL, LIKE I SAID SHE ALWAYS SAT BEHIND THE REJECT, WHICH MEANT THAT SHE ALWAYS HAD TO LOOK AT THE BACK OF HIS **STUPID HEAD** AND HIS **STUPID HAT**.

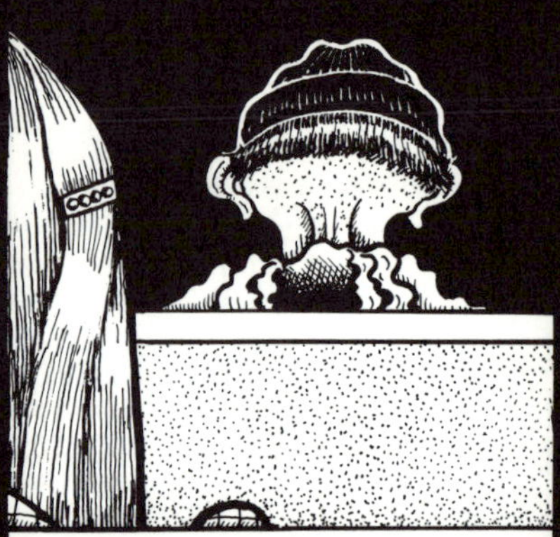

FOR YEARS SHE SAT BEHIND HIM, AND THEY NEVER SAID A WORD TO EACH OTHER, BUT SHE MUST'VE STARTED HAVING **NIGHTMARES** WITH HIM IN IT, BECAUSE ONE DAY SHE JUST **SNAPPED**...

BEFORE ANYONE KNEW WHAT WAS HAPPENING, SHE HAD HER HANDS AROUND HIS SCRAWNY NECK, **SHAKING** AND **CHOKING HIM**, WHILE SHE MADE THESE **WEIRD, SCARY GRUNTING SOUNDS** LIKE THE GIRL IN "THE EXORCIST". THE BUS DRIVER HAD TO **PRY** HER OFF OF HIM AND IT TOOK ABOUT **TEN OF US** TO HOLD HER DOWN UNTIL WE GOT TO THE SCHOOL.

WHEN WE GOT TO SCHOOL ALL THESE **PRINCIPALS** AND **COUNSELLORS** CAME RUNNING OUT AND TOOK HER TO SOME OFFICE. SHE HAD **BLOOD** ALL OVER HER AND SHE WAS COMPLETELY **FLIPPED O-U-T!**

THE REJECT'S NECK WAS BLEEDING, SO THEY **TOOK** HIM TO THE NURSE (HE STILL HAS THE SCARS ON HIS NECK.) BUT HE WAS **LAUGHING** THE WHOLE TIME, LIKE HE THOUGHT IT WAS **FUNNY!** THE **STUPID JERK!**

BUT THE **WEIRD** PART OF ALL THIS IS THAT SHE **STILL SAT BEHIND HIM** FOR THE **REST** OF THE **YEAR!** OH WELL, REJECTS WILL BE REJECTS! **HA HA!**

MY MOTHER SORTA MADE ME BE NICE TO HIM, AND BESIDES, I FELT A LITTLE SORRY FOR HIM*. I MEAN, I'M NOT EXACTLY MR. POPULARITY MYSELF.

BUT MAN, TRYING TO BE FRIENDS WITH THIS KID WAS IMPOSSIBLE! THE FIRST TIME I EVER ASKED HIM TO COME OVER MY HOUSE HE SAID "WHAT FOR?"! AS IF **I** WAS THE **REJECT**!!!

AND WHEN HE DID COME OVER MY HOUSE HE'D DRIVE ME COMPLETELY NUTS! HE WAS ALWAYS* EATING POTATO CHIPS OUT OF HIS COAT POCKET, AND HE'D GET CRUMBS ALL OVER THE FLOOR.

AND HE WAS ALWAYS* WHEEZING AND CHOUGHING AND WIPING HIS SNOTS ON HIS SLEEVE, AND I WAS TERRIFIED OF CATCHING WHATEVER DISEASE IT WAS HE HAD.

AND HE HAD TO TOUCH EVERYTHING! — MY CAR MODELS, MY BASEBALL CARDS, MY COMICS — GETTING HIS SNOTS AND POTATO CHIP GREASE ALL OVER MY VALUABLE STUFF!*

THEN WHEN WE'D PLAY WITH MY TAPE RECORDER HE WOULD ALWAYS GO INTO HIS STUPID "ALL IN THE FAMILY" ROUTINE.

FINALLY ONE DAY HE BUSTED MY TAPE RECORDER AND I TOTALLY BLEW MY COOL. **I COULDN'T TAKE THIS KID ANYMORE!** I JUMPED UP AND STARTED **BASHING HIS HEAD IN!** OF COURSE THAT WAS WHEN MY MOTHER CAME IN AND **I** GOT IN TROUBLE. BUT NEEDLESS TO SAY THAT WAS THE **LAST TIME** THE REJECT CAME OVER **MY** HOUSE!

WE HUNG OUT AT HIS HOUSE A COUPLE OF TIMES BUT THAT WAS EVEN WORSE. HIS HOUSE WAS SPOTLESSLY CLEAN AND YOU WEREN'T ALOUD TO TOUCH ANYTHING. AND HE OWNED NO NEAT STUFF!

WE HAD TO SIT IN THE KITCHEN WITH HIS MOTHER THERE WATCHING US, AND ALL WE'D DO WAS DRAW CARS. AND IT WAS BORING.

HIS PARENTS CAME FROM GERMANY, THOUGH THEY SPOKE PRETTY GOOD AMERICAN. HIS MOTHER WAS STRICT AND KIND OF SCARY, BUT SHE TOLD INTERESTING STORIES.

ONCE SHE TOLD ME ABOUT THE REJECT'S GRANDFATHER, WHO FOUGHT IN AFR- ICA WITH ROMMEL IN WORLD WAR TWO. DROVE A TANK AND EVERYTHING. SOUNDED LIKE A NEAT GUY.
WOW!

SHE WAS ABOUT TO SHOW ME SOME OF HIS OLD WAR SOUVENIRS WHEN THE REJECT WENT INTO A PANIC, BEGGING HIS MOTHER NOT TO SHOW ME THE STUFF.

HE TOOK ME OUTSIDE AND STARTED PLEADING WITH ME NOT TO TELL ANYONE ABOUT HIS GRANDFATHER—THAT HE DID- N'T WANT EVERYONE TO START CALL- ING HIM A NAZI.

I TOLD HIM THAT HE WAS ACTING STUPID, AND THAT HE SHOULD BE PROUD OF HIS GRANDPA, BUT HE SAID THAT HE KNOWS THAT THE GERMANS WERE THE BAD GUYS AND DIDN'T WANT TO BE MADE FUN OF.

I THOUGHT HE WAS GETTING ALL BENT OUT OF SHAPE OVER NOTHING, BUT I KEPT MY MOUTH SHUT. I ALSO DECIDED NOT TO HANG OUT WITH HIM ANYMORE. HE WAS JUST TOO WEIRD. I DIDN'T SEE HIDE NOR HAIR OF HIM ALL THAT SUMMER, UNTIL ONE DAY WHEN ME AND JOEY LARSON WERE HANGING OUT ON THE AQUEDUCT AND WE SAW THE REJECT RUNNING TOWARDS US LIKE A LUNATIC...

HE INSISTED THAT WE GO TO HIS HOUSE, THAT HE HAD SOMETHING HE WANTED TO SHOW US. HE WOULDN'T SAY WHAT IT WAS, JUST THAT IT WAS REALLY "BOSS."

WHEN WE GOT TO HIS HOUSE HE ASKED US TO WAIT OUTSIDE WHILE HE WENT IN TO GET WHATEVER IT WAS HE WANTED TO SHOW US.

FINALLY HE CAME OUT WITH THE "BOSS" SURPRISE: A KITE WITH A PICTURE OF THE INCREDIBLE HULK ON IT. LIKE, BIG FUCKING DEAL!

"OKAY, SO LET US FLY IT"! JOEY SAID, BUT AS SOON AS HE TOUCHED IT THE REJECT GOT ALL UPTIGHT, SAYING HE HAD TO FLY IT FIRST, AND THEN WE COULD HAVE OUR TURNS.

WELL, WE HAD NOTHING ELSE TO DO SO WE SAT DOWN AND LAUGHED WHILE THE REJECT RAN AROUND LIKE A SPAZ TRYING TO GET IT OFF THE GROUND. HE FINALLY MADE IT AFTER ABOUT AN HOUR.

AFTER A WHILE IT WAS MY TURN TO FLY THE KITE, BUT THE WHOLE TIME I WAS HOLDING IT THE REJECT KEPT CLAWING AT ME AND SAYING THAT I WAS GONNA WRECK IT.

NEXT THING YOU KNOW THE KITE GETS STUCK IN A TREE, AND THE REJECT GOES INTO A PANIC. HE YANKED ON THE STRING TOO HARD AND THE KITE CAME DOWN ALL BUSTED UP.

I FELT BAD THAT THE KITE GOT BUSTED— EVEN THOUGH IT WASN'T MY FAULT—SO I STARTED TRYING TO FIX IT, BUT THEN THE REJECT WAS ALL OVER ME, SCREAMING THAT I WRECKED IT AND TO LEAVE IT ALONE.

THAT REALLY PISSED ME OFF—BLAMING ME FOR SOMETHING THAT WAS HIS FAULT— SO I SMASHED HIS KITE INTO A MILLION PIECES...

JOEY LARSON HAD BEEN LAUGHING AT WHAT WAS GOING ON, BUT WHEN THE REJECT STARTED CRYING HE GOT REALLY MAD. HE CALLED HIM A **BIG BABY** AND SAID "I'LL GIVE YOU SOMETHING TO **CRY** ABOUT."

HE PUSHED HIM DOWN AND BEGAN KICKING HIM, AND SOON I JOINED IN. THEN JOEY HAD A BRILLIANT IDEA...

BY NOW THE REJECT WAS **TOTALLY HYSTERICAL.**

THE "CHINESE GRASS TORTURE" IS WHEN YOU STUFF SOMEBODY'S SHIRT AND PANTS WITH **GRASS** (AND STICKS AND LEAVES) 'TIL THEY CAN **HARDLY MOVE.** AND THE ITCHING DRIVES THEM **CRAZY!**

WE FIGURED THAT THIS WOULD **REALLY** MAKE THE REJECT **FREAK-OUT,** BUT Y'KNOW, IT WAS A WEIRD THING... HE DIDN'T CRY OR SCREAM OR MOVE OR DO **ANYTHING.** HE JUST LIED THERE, LIKE HE WAS **DEAD** OR IN A **TRANCE** OR SOMETHING, WHILE WE STUFFED HIS CLOTHES WITH LEAVES, STICKS, ROCKS, EVEN **DOG-SHIT.** *

WELL THIS WAS NO FUN, WITH HIM JUST LYING THERE LIKE A BUMP ON A LOG, SO WE STARTED KICKING HIM AGAIN. THEN I THOUGHT OF CALLING HIM A **NAZI,** FIGURING THAT WOULD GET HIM RILED.

BUT HE JUST LIED THERE WITHOUT MAKING A SOUND.

SO WE DECIDED TO SPLIT. IT WAS GETTING LATE ANYWAYS, SO JOEY AND I SPLIT UP AND HEADED FOR HOME, LEAVING THE REJECT WHERE HE WAS.

ON MY WAY HOME I STARTED THINKING ABOUT THE WEIRD EXPRESSION ON THE REJECTS FACE, AND I COULDN'T HELP WONDERING WHAT HE WAS THINKING JUST NOW.

THAT'S WHEN I HEARD HIM SCREAM, AND THAT PRETTY MUCH ANSWERED MY QUESTION.

WHEN THE NEXT SCHOOL YEAR STARTED HE WASN'T ON OUR BUS, EVEN THOUGH HIS FAMILY STILL LIVED IN THE NEIGHBORHOOD. SOMEONE SAID SOMETHING ABOUT HIS GRANDPA DYING, OR SOMETHING.

IT WASN'T UNTIL NEXT YEAR THAT I SAW HIM AGAIN, AND I BARELY RECOGNIZED HIM*. HE WASN'T MUCH OF A REJECT ANYMORE.

HE DIDN'T HAVE HIS HAT ANYMORE, AND HE WAS ALOT TALLER THAN ME NOW, SO I WASN'T GOING TO MESS WITH HIM. HE ACTED LIKE HE DIDNT RECOGNIZE ME, AND THAT WAS FINE WITH ME.

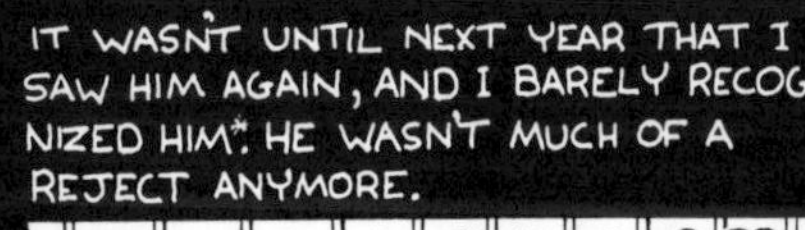

ANYHOW, WE GOT A NEW REJECT ON OUR BUS, NAMED **MIKE POMERANTZ**. YOU SEE, WE DISCOVERED A LITTLE SECRET ABOUT MIKE...

WELL, I DON'T WANT TO GO INTO DETAIL, ALL I'M GONNA TELL YOU IS THAT HIS NICKNAME IS "**ONE-NUT**", AND THAT PRETTY MUCH SAYS IT ALL.

THE   END.

LIFE CAN BE BEAUTIFUL

MY, WHAT A BEAUTIFUL DAY!
YES, BUT IT GRIEVES ME TO THINK THAT ELSEWHERE IN THE WORLD PEOPLE ARE DYING IN HURRICANES AND FLOODS AND TORNADOES!

WHAT A GREAT DAY IT IS TO BE ALIVE!
SIGH LIFE, WHAT A FRAGILE THING! WHY, A HUGE BRANCH COULD FALL OFF THIS TREE AND KILL US ALL IN AN INSTANT!

RYE OR WHOLE WHEAT?
WHOLE WHEAT.
HOW CAN I ENJOY EATING ALL THIS DELICIOUS FOOD KNOWING PEOPLE ARE STARVING ALL OVER THE WORLD!

AHH, THAT WAS GOOD! I'M STUFFED!
OH, WHAT A SPOILED NATION WE ARE, TAKING EVERYTHING FOR GRANTED! I FEEL SO ASHAMED!

C'MON EVERYBODY! LET'S PLAY CATCH!
OKAY!
YES, LET US PLAY NOW WHILE WE STILL CAN, FOR SOMEDAY WE'LL ALL BE TOO OLD AND CRIPPLED WITH ARTHRITIS!

AAAAA AAAAAA AAAAAAA AAAAA
OH MY GOD! JUNIOR JUST FELL OFF A CLIFF AND DIED! BOOHOOHOO!

HEY, DON'T LET IT GET YOU DOWN, HON. JUST TRY TO THINK ABOUT THE GOOD TIMES.
©1987 by PETER BAGGE

BAGGE the MARTYR

"WACKY SAINTS" NUMBER 17 IN A SERIES OF 40. BOTTOMS BUBBLEGUM COMPANY, BROOKLYN, N.Y.